The Pursuit
of Grace

Pastor Kevin Stock

THE PURSUIT OF GRACE

iUniverse books may be ordered through booksellers or by contacting:

iUniverse
1663 Liberty Drive
Bloomington, IN 47403
www.iuniverse.com
844-349-9409

ISBN: 978-1-6632-4583-0 (sc)
ISBN: 978-1-6632-4584-7 (e)

Library of Congress Control Number: 2022917622

Print information available on the last page.

iUniverse rev. date: 09/27/2022

This book is dedicated to Kevin M. (Kev) Stock. A son to be proud of, a brother to be cherished, a husband who was deeply loved, an inspiration as an uncle, cousin and friend. Kev touched the lives of so many during his short time here on earth. He ran the race, he kept the faith, and he fulfilled God's purpose for which he was sent. Kev truly was a mighty oak.

ACKNOWLEDGEMENTS

First of all, I want to thank the Lord for the revelation of His gift of grace to me through His Word and the experiences of my life. Thanks to all who helped on this project as I would never have been able to accomplish this project by himself. I also extend gratitude to my son Kev for his many hours of editing. I thank my son Luke for his illustrations. I also want to thank Francesca Rebottini and also Pastor Frank Todaro for their computer skills as I am pretty much computer illiterate.

CONTENTS

FOREWORD

I have known and been friends with Pastor Kevin for over twenty-five years. For many of those years, he was my pastor. I had the privilege of sitting under his teaching on grace for many years. I have also ministered along side of him on many occasions. I know how much his message of grace has changed my life, and I have also seen many other lives powerfully impacted by this important message.

Contained within the pages of this book are years of revelation that Pastor Stock has received from the Lord. He quotes many Scriptures from both the Old and the New Testaments and ties them together in a way that is easy for the reader to understand. He also intertwines his personal testimony throughout the pages of this book, which further solidifies his teaching on grace, of which he is a major recipient.

I am sometimes amazed at the number of Christians that I meet or minister to who really have no concept or understanding of the message of grace. It is one of the foundational truths of Christianity, yet very few truly grasp this Biblical truth. This book is the remedy for that problem. It provides in great detail all of the many wonderful facets of God's gift of grace.

Pastor Stock reveals man's condition apart from grace; that we were dead in our transgressions and sins and that we were by nature objects of wrath. He shows how mankind tries to remedy this situation by his own efforts, which are not acceptable to God. He then reveals God's remedy for our condition; grace. God Himself has provided everything that man needs to be acceptable in His sight. He did all the work, and the only thing we need to do is receive it by faith.

If you have ever struggled with this issue, or if you are willing to admit that you lack understanding of this important truth, then I highly recommend that you read this book. The truths contained in these pages will clarify any misunderstanding you may have about grace and bring much freedom to your life. It will also reveal God's plan of salvation for mankind, and give you the opportunity to receive it.

Rick Sodmont
Humble Heart Ministries
Associate Pastor, Life Church, Ebensburg, PA

INTRODUCTION

This book is about the grace of God. The title is The Pursuit of Grace. The reason I point out that there is a pursuit involved is because grace is so contrary to what is commonly taught and experienced in the world, our thinking, and unfortunately often times in the church. Therefore, there has to be a constant conscious effort to believe so as to overcome all the opposition to this magnificent gift of God.

Grace is one of the foundational truths of Christianity. When we consider foundations as it relates to building and architecture it is the very first step in the building process. We lay a solid and stable support for the superstructure. Since the entire weight of the structure rests on it; the foundation must be done well, and the taller the building is to be the deeper the foundation must be. Over the years as a pastor, I have discovered that many people within the church don't have a right understanding of foundational truths. As a result, many believers often live a roller coaster Christian life. If we have not mastered the foundational truths, we cannot live a consistent joyful life in Christ.

So, then the purpose of this book is for us to gain a better understanding of this issue of grace, a foundational elementary truth of Christianity.

What must I do to be saved? These are the words of the Philippian jailer to Paul and Silas as recorded in Acts 16. This is the question man has been asking throughout his time here on earth. The very existence of the many different religions found in every nation, tribe, and people group down through the ages attests to the fact that man is indeed concerned about his eternal destination. This is because God has placed eternity within the heart of man, according to the words of Solomon in Ecclesiastes 3:11.

Now being that there are so many different religions and belief systems, it stands to reason that there are many different answers to the question being asked. But what is the truth? What must I do to be saved? I'm sure that everyone thinks that their beliefs are correct, that their answer is the right answer. No one would willingly commit themselves to a belief system that they knew to be erroneous. We don't see churches named the First Church of Deception or watch "The Heresy Hour" on Christian TV. Everyone assumes that their way is the right way. However, in Proverbs 14:12 we're told, *"There is a way that seems right to a man, but in the end, it leads to death."* All religions have a somewhat moral character about them. Most promote good behavior or good works to some degree. They look good, sound good and seem right. But are they true? If not, then they lead to death. So what then is the right way?

In John 14:6 Jesus said, *"I am the way and the truth and the life. No one comes to the Father except through me."* You see Jesus didn't say that there was a plethora of ways in which we might come to God. He said there is only one way, and that is through Him. This is what we want to consider.

CHAPTER 1

Children of Wrath

Colossians 2:8: *See to it that no one takes you captive through hollow and deceptive philosophy, which depends on human tradition and the basic principles of this world rather than on Christ.*

There is an old story about a great king who wanted to obtain all the wisdom of the world. So, he gathered together all of his wise men and assigned them the task of gathering all the pertinent knowledge by which men live. After a year they came back to the king with a large collection of books containing what they believed to be all the wisdom of the world. The king took one look at the books and decided it would take too long to read them all so he told the wise men to condense it down. After many months the wise men returned with one very large volume. Again, the king thought it was still too large and so he asked them if they might condense it more, perhaps down to one line. After many weeks the wise men returned and said to the king; "We have searched throughout the whole earth both far and wide to discover the wisdom by which men live and this is it, your majesty; "There are no free lunches!"

I believe this story sums up what many if not most of us have been taught throughout our lives, nothing is free, everything must be worked for, earned or deserved. Not only does this principle hold true for life in general, but unfortunately for many the same holds true as it relates to one's relationship with God. In the religious system in which I was raised it came across that I was a wretched sinner, that God was angry with me and that I needed to do a great amount of seemingly good works to appease His anger and to be made acceptable in His sight. The actual church building that I was raised in had been built by a local millionaire in the early 1900's. It is a very impressive structure and is recognized by the Vatican as a minor basilica. On the front wall of the sanctuary there is a large painting of Jesus ascending into heaven. While I think Jesus would be beaming, thrilled to be leaving this world and returning to His Father in heaven in the picture He has what almost appears to be a scowl on His face. At least that is how it appeared to me. As I would sit there in church each week looking up at that painting, I knew that that scowl was meant for me. To me God was not *"the compassionate and gracious God slow to anger and abounding in love and faithfulness, forgiving wickedness rebellion and sin,"* as described in Exodus 34:6-7. In my estimation God didn't like me, in fact I was convinced He actually hated me. There was no peace or joy in my life as it related to my relationship with God. Therefore, I looked to other things to find them.

To better understand the need for grace I believe we have to go back to where it all started, back to the very first sin of man in the Garden of Eden.

Genesis 2:16-17: *And the LORD God commanded the man, "You are free to eat from any tree in the garden; 17 but you must not eat from the tree of the knowledge of good and evil, for when you eat of it you will surely die."*

We know what happened, they ate, but they didn't fall over dead, the death wasn't physical, it was spiritual. When Adam and Eve sinned by eating from the Tree of the Knowledge of Good and Evil there were several things that happened. There was a major change that took place in their nature. Whereas they had been created with the very nature of God, now they had a dead fallen nature, a sinful nature, a nature that was in opposition to God, a nature that was independent from and separated from the life of God. That nature has been passed on to the entire human race. Apart from Jesus Christ, every single person born into this world from Adam on has been born with a sinful human nature that is spiritually dead and separated from the life of God; this is our inheritance in Adam. The apostle Paul mentions this spiritual death in several of his epistles.

Ephesians 2:1-3: *As for you, you were dead in your transgressions and sins, 2 in which you used to live when you followed the ways of this world and of the ruler of the kingdom of the air, the spirit who is now at work in those who are disobedient. 3 All of us also lived among them at one time, gratifying the cravings of our sinful nature and following its desires and thoughts. Like the rest, we were by nature objects of wrath.* (NKJV: *children of wrath*).

Colossians 2:13: *When you were dead in your sins and in the uncircumcision of your sinful nature, God made you alive with Christ.*

When Paul stated to the Ephesians and the Colossians that they were dead in their sins it obviously doesn't mean they were physically dead. Paul was not writing his letters to a bunch of corpses. He is pointing out to these believers the spiritual condition that they inherited from Adam. Notice Paul isn't just pointing his finger at others. He includes himself in this; *"All of us also – like the rest we were by nature objects or children of wrath."*

It's important that we see that the transgressions and sins were only the symptoms of a greater cause; *we were by nature objects or children of wrath.*

The root cause of sin and transgression is the fallen nature we've inherited from Adam. We were all born spiritually dead. This is why Jesus told Nicodemus in John 3:3: *"I tell you the truth, no one can see the kingdom of God unless he is born again."* Nicodemus thinking in the physical sense says in verse 4: *"How can a man be born when he is old? Surely, he cannot enter a second time into his mother's womb to be born!"*

Jesus wasn't talking about physical birth; He was referring to spiritual birth. He was pointing out the need for that spiritually dead, fallen nature of man to be brought back into the life of God. It needs to be born of the Spirit. Our inheritance in Adam is that we are born into this world as sinners, before we ever commit an act of sin. Just by our very nature we were under the wrath of God. This is our heredity, this is our spiritual DNA, handed down by Adam.

John 3:36: *Whoever believes in the Son has eternal life, but whoever rejects the Son will not see life, for God's wrath remains on him."*

Notice, *God's wrath remains on him.* Jesus is saying that everyone born into this world is born under the wrath of God and the only means of escape is by being born again through true belief in the Lord Jesus Christ.

This is the only passage in the Johannine Gospel and Epistles in which "wrath" is mentioned. The word does not mean a sudden gust of passion or a burst of temper. Rather, it is the settled displeasure of God against sin. It is the divine allergy to moral evil, the reaction of righteousness to unrighteousness. God is neither easily angered nor vindictive. But by His very nature He is unalterably committed to opposing and judging all disobedience. The moral laws of the universe are as unvarying and unchangeable as its physical laws, and God cannot set aside either without violating His own nature. The rejection of His Son can be followed only by retribution. Acceptance of Christ is the personal appropriation of God's truth and as Jesus says in Jn 8:32; the truth will set you free"
(The Expositors Bible Commentary)

While God considers a person's nature, we as humans always tend to look at behavior. There is a lady in our church who is a couple of years older than me, so basically, we were brought up under the same prevailing culture of our day. After hearing my testimony, a number of times one day she said to me, "I can't even imagine doing the things you did." "I never did any of those things. But I said to her, "Yeah, but we were both going to the same hell." You see, it wasn't my behavior or her behavior it was by our very nature that we were both objects of wrath. Our identity in Adam is sinner! Our identity in Christ is saint! Our identity is not based on our behavior, but rather it is based on our position. We are either in Adam or in Christ. According to the Bible there are only two groups of people in this world; sinners or saints!

In Romans chapter 5 Paul draws a contrast between Adam and Christ.

Romans 5:15-19: *But there is a great difference between Adam's sin and God's gracious gift. For the sin of this one man, Adam, brought death to many. But even greater is God's wonderful grace and his gift of forgiveness to many through this other man, Jesus Christ. 16 And the result of God's gracious gift is very different from the result of that one man's sin. For Adam's sin led to condemnation, but God's free gift leads to our being made right with God, even though we are guilty of many sins. 17 For the sin of this one man, Adam, caused death to rule over many. But even greater is God's wonderful grace and his gift of righteousness, for all who receive it will live in triumph over sin and death through this one man, Jesus Christ. 18 Yes, Adam's one sin brings condemnation for everyone, but Christ's one act of righteousness brings a right relationship with God and new life for everyone. 19 Because one person disobeyed God, many became sinners. But because one other person obeyed God, many will be made righteous.* NLT

Sin and condemnation came through Adam. It comes as an inheritance to all. It is our heredity; we have no choice in the matter. Righteousness and justification on the other hand comes through faith in Christ. We do have a choice! The sin of Adam changed the nature of man, and Adam and Eve also became aware of the effects of their sin.

Genesis 3:7: *Then the eyes of both of them were opened, and they realized they were naked; so, they sewed fig leaves together and made coverings for themselves.*

Immediately upon sinning there was now a sense of guilt and shame; there was now a self-awareness. Their focus was now upon themselves; they became introverted. The self-life had begun! But being that it was *The Tree of the Knowledge of Good and Evil* they knew just what to do. They made garments of fig leaves to cover their nakedness and in doing so this was man's first attempt to cover the guilt, shame and nakedness of his sin. Enter religion. These figs leaves symbolize the essence of works-based religion which says, I've sinned but I can take care of this myself. I can make myself acceptable to God. The erroneous belief that we can earn a right standing in God's sight is the foundation of all of the world's religions. This is also a part of our inheritance in Adam; a works-based mentality. I believe this is intrinsic in the heart of all mankind down through the ages: performance, behavior, works, law, rules, and regulations; religion!

A few examples from scripture: In John 6:28 the people in the crowd who were following after Jesus asked Him, *"What must we do to do the works God requires?"* In Acts 16:30 the Philippian jailer asked Paul and Silas, *"What must I do to be saved?"* Notice in both of these instances the people wanted to know what they had to do in order to be acceptable to God. This is human effort. But this is always how man looks at this issue; "What must I do?" With this mindset the responsibility falls on man. "What do I have to do?" The crowds wanted to know what works they had to do. So, in their estimation it was up to them to somehow perform certain religious works or duties in order to be acceptable to God. But notice what Jesus says to them in response in verse 29, *"The work of God is this; to believe in the one He has sent."*

Jesus didn't tell them to try to be good. He didn't tell them to go to church or strive for perfection. He told them what was pleasing to God was for them to believe in the One He had sent. That was Himself. This is what is pleasing to God; believing God. In fact, that is what faith really is.

When you look at the story of the Philippian jailer in Acts 16:30-31 you see the same thing. The jailer rushes in, throws himself at the feet of Paul and Silas and asks, *"Sirs, what must I do to be saved?"* Paul's answer? Go to church, be good, read your Bible when they eventually become available, be nice to your neighbor? No! he answered, *"Believe on the Lord Jesus Christ and you will be saved."*

I don't think it can be any plainer than this. "What must I do to be saved? Believe on the Lord Jesus Christ and you will be saved." Paul's answer was not for the jailer to do some religious activity or depend on his own efforts. The answer was to believe on the Lord Jesus Christ. The answer to the question is still the same for us today. We can only be saved by truly believing on the Lord Jesus Christ.

Human effort is actually the premise of every single religion on earth. Apart from true Christianity in all of the world's religions there is not one where a person's acceptance by God is based upon what someone else does for them. It is always up to the individual to meet the requirements of that particular religion.

Isaiah 43:10-11: *Before Me there was no God formed, Nor shall there be after Me. 11 I, even I, am the Lord, And besides Me there is no savior.* NKJV

And believe me I needed someone else to do something for me. I needed a savior.

CHAPTER 2

My Story

It was a dark and stormy night. (a cliché' used by Snoopy and many other authors). Somewhere off in the distance a dog barked, a door slammed, a woman screamed, shots rang out and I was born. These words have absolutely nothing to do with this book. I just always wanted to write this. Maybe this will help you better understand what kind of person I am. As a kid growing up, my sense of humor often got me in trouble with my teachers, coaches, priests, nuns, and others in authority over me.

I grew up in a very musical household. We grew up with music playing constantly in our house. When I was 9 years old, I was introduced to the Beatles, I even went to see their movie "A Hard Day's Night." I loved their music, their attitude and their look. As a teenager in the late 60's and early 70's what I embraced the most from the culture of that day was, The Beatles, Woodstock, and Easy Rider. We had a huge poster of Peter Fonda from the movie Easy Rider hanging in our bedroom. By the way my brother and I stole that poster from a gift shop at the Pittsburgh airport. This was the coming of age for sex, drugs and rock n roll.

I was raised outside of a small town in western Pennsylvania. My dad worked in the steel mills in nearby Johnstown. My mother was a stay-at-home mom. We were raised as devout Roman Catholics, as was everyone else that I knew at that time. We attended mass every Sunday and every first Friday of the month. During Lent we observed the Stations of the Cross, and I, like all my friends, attended twelve years of Catholic school. Even though I was raised in a very religious environment, I never had a personal relationship with Jesus Christ. I knew about Him, but I didn't know Him. One of my first recollections of the truth getting through to me was when I was in the second grade. We were being instructed prior to receiving first Holy Communion. My teacher, who was a nun, showed us a picture of Jesus hanging on the cross and told us that Jesus died on the cross for our sin. As I looked at that picture, I thought, "Wow that is so cool, Jesus died for my sins." At that point that truth was planted into my mind. It would be years before it would be planted into my spirit.

One summer night in 1969, when I was fourteen years old, one of my buddies scored four cans of sixteen-ounce lukewarm Pabst Blue Ribbon Beer. We ran down in the woods by the golf course and choked them down. We weren't doing it because we savored its rich robust flavor; we didn't argue over whether it tasted great or was less filling. We did it for one reason only, to get a buzz. It would be years later that the Lord pointed out to me that I opened myself up to a spirit of drunkenness that night. From that point on in my life there was never any such thing as social drinking. I drank for the sole purpose of getting drunk. In years to come, sometimes I would drink till I passed out or until the bars closed and I couldn't get any more beer. It wasn't long till someone showed up with some weed, and I found a new high. This then became my ideal; to get drunk or get high every day. In the years to come it actually was an ideal that was usually attainable. At the time I didn't understand that this ideal was not unique to me. It was a part of fallen mankind's inheritance in Adam.

The Adventures of a Prodigal Son

When I graduated from high school, I went to a heavy equipment school in North Carolina for several months. When I was finished, I came back home and tried to get a job. After several weeks of no success, I called the school and they said that they could get me a job in South Carolina. Thus began my prodigal son adventure. Just like the younger son in the parable, I went to my father and got my inheritance ($200 and a 61 Comet) and set off to a distant country to seek my fortune, South Carolina. I soon discovered that they even spoke a different language there. Within six weeks I was without a job due to partying and missing work. I ended up living in an abandoned house without electricity. Did you ever take a cold bath by candlelight? At about four in the morning a friend and I would hide in the woods beside the local grocery store and wait for the bread truck to make its delivery. In those days grocery stores weren't open 24 hours so they would just put the racks of bread and baked goods right in front of the door. As soon as the truck would leave, we would go steal whatever we could. For weeks I lived on a diet of pinto beans and cinnamon rolls. Instead of coming to my senses and returning back home like the prodigal son in Luke 15, I called my girlfriend back home and asked her to marry me and come join me in this life of luxury. Being incredibly wise and mature for a young girl of 18, naturally she said yes. For me the next 5 years was a constant lifestyle of getting drunk, smoking weed, occasionally doing some acid, THC and magic mushrooms.

CHAPTER 3

The Human Condition

Romans 1:16-17: *I am not ashamed of the gospel, because it is the power of God for the salvation of everyone who believes: first for the Jew, then for the Gentile. 17 For in the gospel a righteousness from God is revealed, a righteousness that is by faith from first to last, just as it is written: "The righteous will live by faith."*

Before plunging into the explanation of this gospel of righteousness Paul takes some time to point out the need for it. In other words, he spends some time explaining the disease before he presents the cure. Paul starts off with God's indictment against the Gentiles;

Romans 1:18-20: *The wrath of God is being revealed from heaven against all the godlessness and wickedness of men who suppress the truth by their wickedness, 19 since what may be known about God is plain to them, because God has made it plain to them. 20 For since the creation of the world God's invisible qualities — his eternal power and divine nature — have been clearly seen, being understood from what has been made, so that men are without excuse.*

In these verses Paul says that God has made Himself known to mankind simply through creation; the very environment that God has placed man in testifies to God's existence. David made this same statement in Psalm 19:1-4: *The heavens declare the glory of God; the skies proclaim the work of his hands. 2 Day after day they pour forth speech; night after night they display knowledge. 3 There is no speech or language where their voice is not heard. 4 Their voice goes out into all the earth, their words to the ends of the world.*

The speech, the language, the voice and, the words are all saying the same thing: I Am Here! This voice and these words go out into all the earth; in others words there is no where we can go on earth to get away from the testimony from nature. This is why all men are without excuse. Even though God made Himself known to man, man chose to reject that knowledge.

Romans 1:21-23: *For although they knew God, they neither glorified him as God nor gave thanks to him, but their thinking became futile and their foolish hearts were darkened. 22 Although they claimed to be wise, they became fools.*

Romans 1:28-32: *Furthermore, since they did not think it worthwhile to retain the knowledge of God, he gave them over to a depraved mind, to do what ought not to be done. 29 They have become filled with every kind of wickedness, evil, greed and depravity. They are full of envy, murder, strife, deceit and malice. They are gossips, 30 slanderers, God-haters, insolent, arrogant and boastful; they invent ways of doing evil; they disobey their parents; 31 they are senseless, faithless, heartless, ruthless. 32 Although they know God's righteous decree that those who do such things deserve death, they not only continue to do these very things but also approve of those who practice them.*

These last five verses point out the end result of man living apart from the knowledge and the guidance of God. The Lord has turned man over to his own devices.

Paul's letters were sent to the first century church. At that time the church was made up of Jews who had converted to Christianity and Gentiles who became believers and came out of paganism. Because of this in some of his letters Paul addresses each group specifically. Starting in chapter two of Romans Paul turns his attention to the Jews.

Romans 2:1-4: *You, therefore, have no excuse, you who pass judgment on someone else, for at whatever point you judge the other, you are condemning yourself, because you who pass judgment do the same things. 2 Now we know that God's judgment against those who do such things is based on truth. 3 So when you, a mere man, pass judgment on them and yet do the same things, do you think you will escape God's judgment? 4 Or do you show contempt for the riches of his kindness, tolerance and patience, not realizing that God's kindness leads you toward repentance?*

Romans 2:8-11: *But for those who are self-seeking and who reject the truth and follow evil, there will be wrath and anger. 9 There will be trouble and distress for every human being who does evil: first for the Jew, then for the Gentile; 10 but glory, honor and peace for everyone*

*who does good: first for the Jew, then for the Gentile. 11 For God does
not show favoritism.*

The point Paul is making here is that the Jews believed they were
in right relationship with God simply because they were Jews. They
had the law and the prophets, the patriarchs, the promises of the
covenant, the sacrificial system, circumcision and the temple where
they believed God resided. After all they were God's chosen people.
In addition to all of that, the Jews had created hundreds of their own
laws that they believed were pleasing to God.

In speaking to the religious leaders of His day, Jesus said in Matthew
15:6-9: *Thus, you nullify the word of God for the sake of your tradition. 7
You hypocrites! Isaiah was right when he prophesied about you: 8 "'These
people honor me with their lips, but their hearts are far from me. 9 They
worship me in vain; their teachings are but rules taught by men.'"*

Here in Romans Paul is basically saying the same thing; that man's
outward religious acts are not what God is concerned with rather it
is the condition of one's heart.

Romans 2:28-29: *A man is not a Jew if he is only one outwardly, nor
is circumcision merely outward and physical. 29 No, a man is a Jew if
he is one inwardly; and circumcision is circumcision of the heart, by the
Spirit, not by the written code. Such a man's praise is not from men,
but from God.*

After pointing out the human condition in chapters one and two
finally in chapter 3 Paul comes to his conclusion; Romans 3:9-12:
*What shall we conclude then? Are we any better? Not at all! We have
already made the charge that Jews and Gentiles alike are all under sin.
10 As it is written: "There is no one righteous, not even one; 11 there*

is no one who understands, no one who seeks God. 12 All have turned away, they have together become worthless; there is no one who does good, not even one."

Thus, the human condition.

CHAPTER 4

Amazing Grace

Nelson's Bible Dictionary defines grace as *Favor or kindness shown without regard to the worth or merit of the one who receives it and in spite of what that same person deserves.* Grace is "unmerited favor." Several years ago, as I was praying the Lord gave me my own my personal definition of grace! He said; "Grace, is you coming to Me with nothing to offer Me, asking Me for everything and I give it to you." Grace is unmerited, unearned, undeserved favor. On the other hand, religion is man attempting to find favor or acceptance with God through following certain rules and regulations. In other words, it's based on man's performance, man's effort, or man's behavior. It's earned, it's deserved, it's worked for, and this is actually the premise of every single religion on earth apart from true Christianity. In the New International Version of the Bible the word grace is used 123 times in the New Testament. It is the foundation, the most elementary truth of the faith. Grace is what makes Christianity unique among the world's religions. Grace as it relates to our initial salvation is the sovereign act of God whereby man is brought into a right relationship with his Creator through the will and action of the Creator.

Long ago there was a very religious man who by his own estimation was faultless. The result of this was a deep desire to persecute and even kill those who did not live up to his standard of holiness. He had already overseen the death and imprisonment of those of another faith, and he was glad to do so. This man's name was Saul and by the grace of God, he was soon to become the Apostle Paul. The apostle Paul has more to say about grace than anyone else in the Bible. He wrote thirteen, possibly fourteen books of the New Testament. He mentions grace in every single one of them. I believe this was because Paul had an understanding of grace like no other New Testament writer. He understood the truth of God's grace because of the experiences of his own life but more importantly through the revelation that was given to him from Jesus Himself regarding this issue. From the experiential side Paul knew what it was like to be shown kindness and favor apart from his deserving it. According to his own testimony in Acts 22:3-5 Paul says: *Under Gamaliel I was thoroughly trained in the law of our fathers and was just as zealous for God as any of you are today. 4 I persecuted the followers of this Way to their death, arresting both men and women and throwing them into prison, 5 as also the high priest and all the Council can testify. I even obtained letters from them to their brothers in Damascus, and went there to bring these people as prisoners to Jerusalem to be punished.*

In Acts 26:9-17 Paul is brought before King Agrippa, there he says; *"I too was convinced that I ought to do all that was possible to oppose the name of Jesus of Nazareth. 10 And that is just what I did in Jerusalem. On the authority of the chief priests, I put many of the saints in prison, and when they were put to death, I cast my vote against them. 11 Many a time I went from one synagogue to another to have them punished, and I tried to force them to blaspheme. In my obsession against them, I even went to foreign cities to persecute them.*

As I consider Paul's testimony, I get a picture of God with arms folded looking down on him from heaven and saying, "You know what? I've had just about enough of this guy." BAM! "I'm going to save him." I always said it's a good thing I'm not God or we'd be missing about half of the New Testament. (That's what Paul ended up writing.)

Instead of being squashed like a bug by God, Paul continues; *"On one of these journeys I was going to Damascus with the authority and commission of the chief priests. About noon, O king, as I was on the road, I saw a light from heaven, brighter than the sun, blazing around me and my companions. 14 We all fell to the ground, and I heard a voice saying to me in Aramaic, 'Saul, Saul, why do you persecute me? It is hard for you to kick against the goads.' 15 "Then I asked, 'Who are you, Lord?' "'I am Jesus, whom you are persecuting,' the Lord replied. 16' Now get up and stand on your feet. I have appeared to you to appoint you as a servant and as a witness of what you have seen of me and what I will show you. 17 I will rescue you from your own people and from the Gentiles. I am sending you to them 18 to open their eyes and turn them from darkness to light, and from the power of Satan to God, so that they may receive forgiveness of sins and a place among those who are sanctified by faith in me.'*

Consider Paul's spiritual condition as he traveled on that road to Damascus. He was filled with hatred, violence and by his own account he was guilty of murder. Paul hated Jesus and was out to kill or imprison Jesus' people. His behavior certainly did not warrant his being accepted into the kingdom of God. Not exactly the type of person we would expect to be found favorable in God's estimation. And yet we see the Lord's response to him: *I have appeared to you to appoint you as a servant and as a witness of what you have seen of me and what I will show you.*

Later on in 1Timothy 1:12-16 Paul writes: *"I thank Christ Jesus our Lord, who has given me strength, that He considered me faithful, appointing me to His service.* God saw Paul as being faithful even while He was opposed to Jesus, and was not yet converted himself. For *God calls the things that are not as though they are.* Romans 4:17

In verses 13-16 Paul goes on to say: *Even though I was once a blasphemer and a persecutor and a violent man, I was shown mercy because I acted in ignorance and unbelief. 14 The grace of our Lord was poured out on me abundantly, along with the faith and love that are in Christ Jesus. 15 Here is a trustworthy saying that deserves full acceptance: Christ Jesus came into the world to save sinners — of whom I am the worst. 16 But for that very reason I was shown mercy so that in me, the worst of sinners, Christ Jesus might display His unlimited patience as an example for those who would believe on Him and receive eternal life.*

To me this seems like God was looking for the worst possible person He could find to use as an example of His unlimited, unconditional, mercy, grace, and love. So, in essence Paul is God's display model for others to see so that they would not think any were beyond God's redemption. It's interesting that the worst of sinners wasn't a member of Hell's Angels, or the Nazi commandant of an extermination camp during the Holocaust or a member of ISIS who cuts off the heads of children with a knife. The worst of sinners was a religious zealot who claimed "as for legalistic righteousness I was faultless." Philippians 3:6

Paul wasn't looking for God, he thought he already knew Him. Surely God was pleased with him. But His ways are not our ways. It wasn't Paul's efforts that made him acceptable to God. It wasn't his religion, it wasn't his behavior, it wasn't his obedience, and it wasn't his performance. In fact, all of these would actually seem to be the very things that would keep him from being pleasing to God. Simply put, it was a display of God's grace; giving him something that he was totally undeserving of. But that is the very nature of grace. I think Paul sums this up best where he quotes Isaiah 65:1 in Romans 10:20. *"And Isaiah boldly says, "I was found by those who did not seek me; I revealed myself to those who did not ask for me."* Paul knew this scripture to be true through the experience of his own life. So, do I.

CHAPTER 5

Life Goes On

After moving back home to Pennsylvania we had our first two sons, but that didn't slow me down any. I was living completely for myself. My goal in life was to get drunk or get high. At this time, I was working in an underground coal mine. One night I was working hoot owl, the 12am to 8am shift. Before going to work that evening, I drank 10 cans of beer and smoked 3 joints. I then went to work underground where I ran a piece of equipment called a shuttle car or buggy. It hauled about 8-10 tons of coal. The section where I was working that night was about 4 feet high. I was literally bouncing that machine off the walls that night. It was only by the grace of God that I didn't kill myself or someone else. This was my spiritual condition at that time.

I had an older brother, who has since passed away. We were only eleven months apart in age, so for three weeks each year we were the same age. Growing up we were very close. His real name was Dennis but in high school he got the nickname Woodstock which was then changed to Woody. Woody was a lot bigger than me; he was about 6 foot 180 pounds and he was a fighter. In his early twenties, he was single, he worked in the mines so he always had lots of money, some good weed, a Harley, fast women, and he carried a gun. In my estimation he was living the dream. Woody's idea of a good time was going into a bar where there were only three or four guys and beating them up and throwing them out so that he could sit at the bar and drink by himself.

In December of 1977 he went into the local bar and got into a fight with three guys. During the fight he had an out of body experience where he was outside of himself looking down and watching as he went berserk on those guys. What he saw horrified him. He saw himself in a blind rage, screaming, and totally out of control. Two of them managed to get away from him and ran out the door. He had the third one by the hair and was slamming his head off the floor. The bartender who was a friend of ours came out from behind the bar and whacked Woody across the back with a night stick. When he rolled off the guy, the bartender told the other guy to get out of there. When Woody regained his senses, he jumped up and ran out to his truck to get his gun as he was going to kill them. Fortunately, however, they had already taken off.

Back up a few months. Woody worked as a roof bolter in the mines and his partner (or as we would say in the mines his "buddy") was a Christian. He would sometimes witness to Woody. One day when he shared something Woody said, "Where are you getting all this stuff, you're telling me?" The guy said, "In the Bible." Then he asked Woody, "Do you have a Bible?" Woody said, "No." The guy said, "Would you like one?" Woody said, "Yeah, I'll take yours." The guy said, "I'll get you a new one." "No, I want yours." "But mine is all marked up and taped together; I'll get you a new one." "I don't want a new one, I want yours." So, the guy gave him his Bible. Over the course of the next few months Woody read Matthew, Mark, Luke, John, Acts and was half way through the book of Romans. Fast forward to that December night in the bar. After seeing that the three guys had split Woody drove his truck back out to the farmhouse where he was living. His out of body experience had deeply rattled him. He took out his gun, put it to his head and said, "God, if this born-again thing that this guy has been telling me about is for real then you've got do something because I can't go on living like this. So much for living the dream. BANG! Not the gun! Instant transformation! Radical salvation! As Paul states in 2Corinthians 5:17: *Therefore, if anyone is in Christ, he is a new creature; the old things passed away; behold, new things have come.*

My brother was living proof of that verse. No more drunkenness, no more drugs, no more womanizing, no more fights, although he did go back into the bar and tried to preach. A few times when someone wouldn't listen, he'd grab them by the collar put them up against the wall and read scripture to them. Funny, he didn't get too many converts that way. In all honesty I thought he had a mental breakdown. He just wasn't the same guy. He then tried to get me to start going to church with him. I thought, "You're nuts; I've gone to church all my life and it never did anything for me."

The Charismatic movement in the Catholic Church was going on big time in our area in those days. Woody became involved in it and asked me to come with him to their meetings. I disrespectfully declined. In November of 1978 I went on a hunting trip with my dad and my three brothers. I rode in the car with Woody and my brother Gary. As we traveled along, I sat and drank beer while they discussed different passages from the Book of Revelation. At one point they mentioned the lake of fire. I had often heard of hell growing up, but I had never heard that particular term. Over the next few months, I would get a mental picture of a lake of fire, and I realized that was where I was going. Right about this time my wife Sue had a miscarriage and spent several days in the hospital. It was at that time that the Lord began to get hold of her heart. Mine was still as hard as ever.

CHAPTER 6

For the Love of God

Ephesians 2:1-5: *As for you, you were dead in your transgressions and sins, 2 in which you used to live when you followed the ways of this world and of the ruler of the kingdom of the air, the spirit who is now at work in those who are disobedient. 3 All of us also lived among them at one time, gratifying the cravings of our sinful nature and following its desires and thoughts. Like the rest, we were by nature objects of wrath. 4 But because of his great love for us, God, who is rich in mercy, 5 made us alive with Christ even when we were dead in transgressions — it is by grace you have been saved.*

A person who is dead is unable to do anything for themselves. That is exactly where we were spiritually; dead, and therefore unable to do anything to change our situation. After pointing out in Eph 2 that we were all dead in our transgressions and sins, that we were following the ways of the world, that we were under the influence of the ruler of the kingdom of the air, and that we were by nature objects of God's wrath, in verses 4-5 Paul makes an amazing statement. *"But because of His great love for us, God, who is rich in mercy, 5 made us alive with Christ even when we were dead in transgressions — it is by grace you have been saved."*

The word "but" is a conjunction, a grammatical word used in the middle of or at the beginning of a sentence to introduce something that is true in spite of either being or seeming contrary to what has just been said. Consider what had just been said; *We were dead in our trespasses and sins; we followed the ways of this world; we were under the influence of the ruler of the power of the air; we lived our lives gratifying the desires of our sinful nature and we were by nature objects of wrath. But because of His great love for us, God, who is rich in mercy, made us alive with Christ even when we were dead in transgressions — it is by grace you have been saved.*

But because of His great love for us. Talk about something being contrary to what had just been said. He gives His great love not because of our great love for Him, not because we deserved it, not because He owed us anything, not because of our behavior, not because of our goodness, not because of our good works, not because there was something inherently good in us, not because of our observance of religion; not because our good deeds outweigh the bad. *But because of His great love for us!*

These verses show that God takes the initiative. It is because of His great love for us. God's love, unlike our human love is unconditional. The Greek word to describe God's love for us is agape. Vine's

Expository Dictionary of New Testament Words defines it as; *Not the love of complacency, or affection, that is, it was not drawn out by any excellency in its objects, Romans 5:8.* It was an exercise of the divine will in deliberate choice, made without assignable cause save that which lies in the nature of God Himself. *(Vine's Expository Dictionary of Biblical Words),*

Romans 5:8: *But God demonstrates his own love for us in this: While we were still sinners, Christ died for us.*

Agape love is the unconditional love of God towards man. God has made a conscious, deliberate choice to love us in spite of ourselves.

Titus 3:3-5: *At one time we too were foolish, disobedient, deceived and enslaved by all kinds of passions and pleasures. We lived in malice and envy, being hated and hating one another. 4 But when the kindness and love of God our Savior appeared, 5 He saved us, not because of righteous things we had done, but because of His mercy.*

John 3:16: *"For God so loved the world that He gave His only begotten Son, that whoever believes in Him should not perish but have everlasting life. 17 For God did not send His Son into the world to condemn the world, but that the world through Him might be saved.* NKJV

When I consider these verses, I often think of God up in heaven looking down at mankind throughout the ages. What does He see? Some basically good people who just haven't reached their full potential? Capable beings who have not yet worked their way to enlightenment? No, He sees the Spanish Inquisition, the Nazi Holocaust, ethnic cleansing in Bosnia and Rwanda, the horrors of WWII, millions upon millions of abortions, pedophiles, homosexuals, adulterers, hookers, pimps, liars, murderers, thieves, and drunkards. He sees hatred, greed, corruption, self-righteousness, and rebellion; He sees you and me. So how can God so love the world? Obviously, it doesn't have to do with any merit on man's part. There is nothing about man that would warrant God's love for us. God made a conscious, deliberate choice to love the human race in spite of ourselves. This is the essence of grace.

1 John 4:16: *And so we know and rely on the love God has for us. God is love.*

We have come to know and have believed the love which God has for us. God is love. NAS

This verse points out that the nature of God is not some angry, vindictive tyrant who takes pleasure in destroying those who are disobedient. He doesn't just have love; He is love. But as John points out we need a revelation of that love.

And we know (understand, recognize, are conscious of, by observation and by experience) and believe (adhere to and put faith in and rely on) the love God cherishes for us. God is love. AMP

There is a book entitled; The Knowledge of the Holy by A.W.Tozer. The title of chapter one is; Why We Must Think Rightly About God. Tozer asks the question; "What comes into our minds when we think about God is the most important thing about us. For this reason, the gravest question before the Church is always God Himself, and the most portentous fact about any man is not what he at any given time may say or do, but what he in his deep heart conceives God to be like. We tend by a secret law of the soul to move toward our mental image of God. Were we able to extract from any man a complete answer to the question, "What comes into your mind when you think about God?" we might predict with certainty the spiritual future of that man."
(The Knowledge of the Holy, Aiden Wilson Tozer)

So, what is our mental image of God? How we see Him will determine how we respond to Him. One of my favorite verses in scripture is Exodus 34:5-7. The reason I like it so much is that this is not man trying to describe God, rather it is God describing Himself to man; in other words, this is God saying, "This is who I am."

Exodus 34:5-7: *Then the Lord came down in the cloud and stood there with him and proclaimed his name, the Lord. 6 And he passed in front of Moses, proclaiming, "The Lord, the Lord, the compassionate and gracious God, slow to anger, abounding in love and faithfulness, 7 maintaining love to thousands, and forgiving wickedness, rebellion and sin.*

Contrary to popular belief, God does not take pleasure in punishing anyone.

Ezekiel 33:11: *As surely as I live, declares the Sovereign Lord, I take no pleasure in the death of the wicked, but rather that they turn from their ways and live.*

Ezekiel 18:32: *For I take no pleasure in the death of anyone, declares the Sovereign Lord. Repent and live!*

2 Peter 3:9: *The Lord is not wanting anyone to perish, but everyone to come to repentance.*

God is love and His desire is for everyone to come to Him.

Paul goes on in Ephesians 2:8-9 to say: *For it is by grace you have been saved, through faith — and this not from yourselves, it is the gift of God— 9 not by works, so that no one can boast.*

Notice that Paul points out that salvation is a gift. We know that when we give a gift to a person, we don't give them the bill as well. (Unless it is our kids giving us a gift). Gifts are given freely.

Romans 4:4-5: *Now when a man works, his wages are not credited to him as a gift, but as an obligation. 5 However, to the man who does not work but trusts God who justifies the wicked, his faith is credited as righteousness.*

Both of these passages speak of a gift which is freely received and work which is by one's own effort. Even though the Lord tells us that our salvation is a free gift man has a tendency to want to work his way to heaven.

There is a scripture that I believe is most often quoted out of context.

Isaiah 55:8-9 says, *"For my thoughts are not your thoughts, neither are your ways my ways," declares the LORD. 9 "As the heavens are higher than the earth, so are my ways higher than your ways and my thoughts than your thoughts.*

We often use this passage to show that there are times in which God works out circumstances and situations in our lives in ways in which we would never have imagined. While we thought of things turning out in a certain way, the Lord works things out in ways we would never have thought of. And so, we conclude then that His ways and His thoughts are much greater than ours. While it is certainly true that He does work in this way sometimes that is not the primary point of this passage. For when you put it into its proper context you see that this passage is really talking about salvation by grace.

Isaiah 55:1-3: *Come, all you who are thirsty, come to the waters; and you who have no money, come, buy and eat! Come, buy wine and milk without money and without cost. 2 Why spend money on what is not bread, and your labor on what does not satisfy? Listen, listen to me, and eat what is good, and your soul will delight in the richest of fare. 3 Give ear and come to me; hear me, that your soul may live. I will make an everlasting covenant with you, my faithful love promised to David. .*

Notice, first of all, the invitation to come. The Lord is inviting us to come to Him. Then He makes an astounding statement. He says if you are thirsty or hungry, you can come and buy water, wine, milk and bread without money and without cost. Try that the next time you go to Wal-Mart. Just load up your cart and head for your car. I'm sure they will understand. After all the Lord says we can. But really what the Lord is saying here is that His way of salvation is different than what man expects.

In verses. 6-7 it continues, *"Seek the LORD while he may be found; call on Him while He is near. 7 Let the wicked forsake his way and the evil man his thoughts. Let him turn to the LORD, and He will have mercy on him, and to our God, for He will freely pardon.*

Several other translations of the Bible say, "He will abundantly pardon." This is not an overlooking of a few minor infractions, but an abundance of pardon. We see here the crux of this passage. Turn to Me and I will have mercy on you and I will freely pardon you. This is the true context of this passage. It's about how to come to God, and what He will do for us. It then moves into verses. 8-9: *"For My thoughts are not your thoughts, neither are your ways My ways,"* declares the LORD. *"As the heavens are higher than the earth, so are My ways higher than your ways and My thoughts than your thoughts."*

The bottom line in all of this, is that the Lord is telling us that being made right with Him, being acceptable to Him, being saved, receiving eternal life, going to heaven, regardless of what terminology we might use to express it, is not based on the way mankind naturally thinks it is. Man sees it as, "What must I do?" Whereas God says I already did it for you!"

CHAPTER 7

From Darkness to Light

In April of 1979 Woody once again invited me to go to the charismatic meetings with him. They were having a six-week program called Life in the Spirit. It was every Friday night at the Catholic high school that I had attended. There were several nuns and a priest who were teaching about the Person and the work of the Holy Spirit. It was at about this same time that my wife Sue said she wanted a divorce as I was drunk almost every day. I knew things were not good, yet I did nothing to change. I really didn't care. Then one day Woody told me that if I would go to these classes, he would give me one of his cars. I had an old beat-up Volkswagen, and I needed a car.

I was working in the mines, and we worked swing shifts so every third week I was working second shift which was from four in the afternoon till midnight. I had it figured out that on those weeks I had a valid excuse not to go to the meetings so I would only have to go to four of those classes. The first night Sue and I went to class; same high school, same class rooms. A nun spent about an hour teaching about the person and the work of the Holy Spirit. I was clueless as to what she was talking about. In my upbringing in the Catholic Church, I had heard very little about the Holy Spirit. It was kind of like being back in high school. I just sat there nodding my head like I knew what she was talking about. Yeah, it was just like being back in high school.

After class that first night we went upstairs to the school library for a prayer meeting. There were about sixty people who showed up. There were four or five people with guitars, and we started singing some choruses. I actually thought, "Hey this isn't too bad." But then some of them began to sing in tongues, and I checked out. I thought I may be a drunk but these people are all nuts. However, I continued to go back each week as I needed that car. One Friday night we went, and when it was over, I took Sue home, rolled a couple of joints, and went down to the bar till about three in the morning. This is where I was spiritually. *"I was found by those who did not seek me; I revealed myself to those who did not ask for me."*

On the last night of the classes, we were taken into the chapel at the high school to be prayed for. Two nuns and a priest laid hands on me (not the way they had done when I was goofing off in grade school). No, this was different; they began to pray for me to be filled with the Holy Spirit. I wasn't even saved! There was no talk of being born again, no deep repentance, no sinner's prayer. They began to pray and BAM, I got saved, filled with the Holy Spirit, and began to speak in tongues in that order all in about fifteen seconds of each other. Incredibly the same thing happened to Sue that same night.

Over the years I have considered the blessing of us both coming to God at the same time as I have seen the struggle so many have when only either the husband or the wife is saved and are unequally yoked. I walked out of that chapel that night with an incredible sense of peace and joy, feeling as though the weight of the world had been lifted off of me. All I knew was that when I died, I was going to heaven because Jesus died for my sins even though salvation through the blood of Jesus was never mentioned; the teachings had only focused on the Holy Spirit. I didn't even know what it was called. About six months later I was telling someone what had happened to me and they said, "You got saved." I said, "Is that what it's called?" I had never really heard that expression before. *"I was found by those who did not seek me; I revealed myself to those who needed a free car."* The Stock Translation. Not only did I get the car, a 1972 Plymouth Satellite Sebring, but the Lord restored Sue's love for me as well. I don't exactly remember the timeline but not too long prior to the events of May 18ᵗʰ Sue said she wanted a divorce. That all changed really quick. In fact, it was so strong that it kind of scared me. She just couldn't keep her hands off of me. RRRRROW!

So how did this happen? Paul says in Ephesians 1:13-14: *And you also were included in Christ when you heard the word of truth, the gospel of your salvation. Having believed, you were marked in Him with a seal, the promised Holy Spirit, 14 who is a deposit guaranteeing our inheritance.*

You were included in Christ, you were saved, you were born again, you were converted, whatever terminology you might use, they all mean the same thing. Notice Paul says we were included in Christ when we heard the word of truth, the gospel of our salvation and believed it. Up until this point I had not only heard the gospel every time I went to Mass, but I spoke it. At every Mass we recited the Apostle's Creed which says; *We believe in one Lord, Jesus Christ, the only Son of God, eternally begotten of the Father, God from God, Light from Light, true God from true God, begotten not made, one in being with the Father. Through Whom all things were made. For us men and for our salvation He came down from heaven; by the power of the Holy Spirit, He was born of the Virgin Mary, suffered under Pontius Pilate was crucified, died and was buried. On the third day He rose again in fulfillment of the scriptures; He ascended into heaven and is seated at the right hand of the Father. He will come again in glory to judge the living and the dead and His kingdom will have no end.*

Right, there is the word of truth, the gospel of our salvation. Jesus is God, He came down from heaven, He became man, for our salvation He was crucified, He was raised from the dead in fulfillment of scripture, He ascended into heaven, He is coming back again as judge, and His kingdom will have no end. These words were so pounded into me as a kid that even to this day I can recite these words verbatim from memory. Every time I went to mass I not only heard these words but I also spoke these words.

Proverbs 18:21: *Death and life are in the power of the tongue,* NKJV

Even though I spoke those words of life I didn't actually believe them.

Just recently the Lord pointed something out to me; In John 6:63 Jesus said, *"The Spirit gives life; the flesh counts for nothing. The words I have spoken to you are spirit and they are life.*

The flesh counts for nothing. I had those words from the Apostles Creed memorized in my mind (my flesh), although they were true, they counted for nothing. On that Friday night in May of 1979, however, when those nuns and that priest laid hands on me the Holy Spirit took that word of truth that was implanted in my mind (that is, in my flesh), breathed the breath of life upon them (the Spirit), and they became a living reality. I once heard a preacher say that there are people who miss heaven by eighteen inches. That is the approximate distance between your heart and your brain. We can have the knowledge of the truth in our head (intellectually) but not have it in our hearts, meaning faith.

In referring to the children of Israel in the wilderness the writer of Hebrews says, *"For we also have had the gospel preached to us, just as they did; but the message they heard was of no value to them, because those who heard did not combine it with faith."* Hebrews 4:2

The message has no benefit if it is not appropriated by faith. The church that I pastor hears this all the time; what I say is the greatest revelation God ever gave me; "Knowin' Ain't Doin'". That's just how He said it to me. Someone once told me that when God speaks to us, He speaks to us the same way that we speak; if that's true then God talks to people from Alabama with a Southern drawl. To me He said, "Knowin' Ain't Doin'." I guess a more refined way of saying it would be "revelation without application is just useless information." Just knowing what the Word says without believing it in faith does not produce life.

Ephesians 2:8-9: *For it is by grace you have been saved, through faith — and this not from yourselves, it is the gift of God— 9 not by works, so that no one can boast.*

As we can see from these verses we are saved by grace. But we are not saved by grace alone. We are saved by grace through faith. Faith is what activates that grace. Faith is what makes grace a living reality.

There is an old saying that says; "You can sit in a garage for 40 years and never turn into a car, and you can sit in a church for 40 years and never become a believer." Simply hearing is not believing.

Romans 5:1-2: *Therefore, since we have been justified through faith, we have peace with God through our Lord Jesus Christ, 2 through whom we have gained access by faith into this grace in which we now stand.*

Notice it says we have gained access into grace through faith, not by works or religion or anything else.

Titus 2:11: *For the grace of God that brings salvation has appeared to all men.*

This verse is saying that salvation through grace is available to all mankind. Does that mean that all mankind will be saved? When I mention this verse in preaching or teaching on grace, I always ask this question: if you are in a submarine three hundred feet under the water are you in the water? I always get a laugh at the same dumb looks on people's faces. The truth is you are in the water, you are surrounded by the water, but the water is not touching you. It's the same way with grace. It has appeared to all men; therefore, we are surrounded by the grace of God. In fact, I believe we are immersed in an ocean of God's grace, His mercy, and His love, and yet it may not touch us. There has to be a faith response. The Beatles were right, "We all live in a yellow submarine."

Isaiah 26:10 tells us that even though grace is available to all men not all will respond to it. *Though grace is shown to the wicked, they do not learn righteousness; even in a land of uprightness they go on doing evil and regard not the majesty of the Lord.*

We are also told in Ephesians 2:8 that God is giving us a gift. So, what is the gift that's mentioned here? Obviously, it is salvation. Our salvation is a free gift from God. But the gift is also grace, and it is also faith as well. Something the Lord pointed out to me recently is that faith is the God- given ability for us to be able to believe. So, faith itself is a gift from God. God gives us the ability to believe, but it's the Word of God that tells us what to believe. Faith must be based in truth. The Word is truth.

Romans 10:12-15: *For there is no difference between Jew and Gentile — the same Lord is Lord of all and richly blesses all who call on him, 13 for, "Everyone who calls on the name of the Lord will be saved." 14 How, then, can they call on the one they have not believed in? And how can they believe in the one of whom they have not heard? And how can they hear without someone preaching to them? 15 And how can they preach unless they are sent? As it is written, "How beautiful are the feet of those who bring good news!"*

In these verses Paul points out that people need to hear the gospel, the word of truth in order to be saved. Faith must be based on truth. But he goes on to say in verses 16-17: *But not all the Israelites accepted the good news. For Isaiah says, "Lord, who has believed our message?" Consequently, faith comes from hearing the message, and the message is heard through the word of Christ.*

True faith is simply believing what God says. The Philippian jailer in Acts 16 asked Paul and Silas "What must I do to be saved?" Paul answered, "Believe on the Lord Jesus Christ and you will be saved." Vines Expository Dictionary of New Testament Words defines the word "believe" as it is used in the New Testament to mean: *"to be persuaded of," "to place confidence in, to trust," complete reliance upon, not mere credence.* By believing in Jesus, we do not simply believe that He was a real person who lived on earth a couple of thousand years ago. It is not just believing He was a great prophet or teacher here to instruct us on how to live a good moral life. We must believe what He said about Himself; John 14:6-7: *"I am the way and the truth and the life. No one comes to the Father except through Me. 7 If you really knew Me, you would know My Father as well.*

True belief is coming to the place where we give up on our own self effort to be acceptable to God and put our complete trust in the sacrifice Jesus made for us. It is believing that Jesus took our sin upon Himself and took the full punishment that you and I deserve. It is believing that my salvation is dependent on someone other than myself.

Isa 53:4-6: *Surely, He took up our infirmities and carried our sorrows, yet we considered Him stricken by God, smitten by Him, and afflicted. 5 But He was pierced for our transgressions, He was bruised for our iniquities; the punishment that brought us peace was upon Him, and by His wounds we are healed. 6 We all, like sheep, have gone astray, each of us has turned to his own way; and the Lord has laid on Him the iniquity of us all.*

I personally believe that the Father began to download the iniquity of the entire human race onto Jesus in the Garden of Gethsemane. Is it any wonder then than He began to literally sweat blood?

CHAPTER 8

A New Creature

Ephesians 1:13-14: *And you also were included in Christ when you heard the word of truth, the gospel of your salvation. Having believed, you were marked in Him with a seal, the promised Holy Spirit, 14 who is a deposit guaranteeing our inheritance.*

Here God promises that when one hears the gospel of salvation and truly believes it; when one truly puts faith in Christ, not only are we saved, but the Holy Spirit then comes and indwells that individual. The Spirit of God comes and gives life to our dead spirit.

2 Corinthians 1:21-22: *Now it is God who makes both us and you stand firm in Christ. He anointed us, 22 set His seal of ownership on us, and put His Spirit in our hearts as a deposit, guaranteeing what is to come.*

1 Corinthians 6:17: *But he who is joined to the Lord is one spirit with Him.*
NKJV

As a believer our spirit has been redeemed as it has become one with the Spirit of God. As God sees us spiritually, He sees that His Spirit has been joined to our spirit. Therefore, He sees us as holy and blameless. That is our position with Him. However, our soul and our body have not yet been redeemed although at some point they will be. Our soul consists of our mind, our emotions and our free will.

In Ezekiel 36 the Lord gives us a prophetic picture of the new birth.

Ezekiel 36:25-27: *I will sprinkle clean water on you, and you will be clean; I will cleanse you from all your impurities and from all your idols. 26 I will give you a new heart and put a new spirit in you; I will remove from you your heart of stone and give you a heart of flesh. 27 And I will put my Spirit in you and move you to follow my decrees and be careful to keep my laws.*

God says that when He puts His Spirit in us His Spirit then begins to lead us and empower us to live a new life. Because the Holy Spirit is Holy, He leads us toward holiness. This is the process of sanctification which we will consider later on.

Prior to coming to Christ my heart's desire was to get drunk or high every day. On May 18th something radically changed. Even though I still tried to engage in those past activities somehow, they weren't the same. I didn't realize for some time that it was actually the Holy Spirit in me leading me on the right path just as it says in Ezekiel

36. His leading didn't come in a condemning kind of way, but in a gentler, "You don't really need that stuff," kind of way.

2 Corinthians 5:17: *Therefore, if anyone is in Christ, he is a new creature; the old things passed away; behold, new things have come.* NASU

A woman once told me that I had the foulest mouth of anyone she had ever been around. Hey, come on, I was a coalminer. Someone once said it took coalminers a lot longer to say something because of how many F- bombs were used in saying it. We often put the F-bomb in the middle of other words. But after that Friday night, that instantly disappeared; the next day, Saturday May 19ᵗʰ I could no longer cuss. The Lord delivered me from that sin instantly. I wished that had been the case with a whole lot of other things as well. It wasn't until later on that I began to understand what was happening with me. Not only was I saved by grace, but grace was also doing another work in me.

Titus 2:11-14: *For the grace of God that brings salvation has appeared to all men. 12 It teaches us to say "No" to ungodliness and worldly passions, and to live self-controlled, upright and godly lives in this present age, 13 while we wait for the blessed hope — the glorious appearing of our great God and Savior, Jesus Christ, 14 who gave himself for us to redeem us from all wickedness and to purify for himself a people that are his very own, eager to do what is good.*

Grace is the character of God Himself, we are saved by grace but grace is also the power of God for us to live a godly life. Even though the Spirit and the power of grace were leading me toward godliness, my flesh still wanted to continue in its old ways. After the events of May 18ᵗʰ, we continued to go to the charismatic prayer meetings on Friday nights. One night when we came home, I took my weed and threw it in the garbage can. The next morning, I was rooting through the garbage looking for it thinking, "What were you thinking?" I was starting to experience what Paul describes in Galatians 5, the struggle between the Spirit and the flesh which is our soul. Some within the Body of Christ believe that if there are not a bunch of laws, rules and regulations to keep people in line, then people will just live like hell with no restraints. This is why the Ten Commandments are so often emphasized. We have to keep the people in line. In 2Cororinthians 3:7 Paul referred to the Ten Commandments as the ministry that brought death. They brought death because no one was able to live up to them. Why would we try to live up to them today? The church still believes we need them as a means of restraint for believers. So, what then was the purpose of the law? Without going into detail let me just briefly state two verses.

Romans 3:20: *through the law we become conscious of sin.*

Through the law, which includes the ten commandments God shows us what sin is. Knowing then what sin is the law also convicts us when we break it.

Galatians 3:24: *the law was put in charge to lead us to Christ that we might be justified by faith.*

The intent of the law is also to lead a person to Christ. It points out our need for the Savior as we are unable to keep the demands of the law in and of ourselves.

As we've seen so far, God has put His Spirit in us, and His Spirit moves us to follow His decrees and to be careful to keep His laws. In Titus 2:12 we're told that grace teaches us to say "No" to ungodliness and worldly passions, and to live self-controlled, upright and godly lives in this present age. Then there is the Word of God as well.

Ps 119:9,11: *How can a young man keep his way pure? By living according to your word. 11 I have hidden your word in my heart that I might not sin against you.*

We have become a new creature indwelt with the Holy Spirit, we have the power of grace teaching us to say no to ungodliness, and we have the Word of God leading us into the truth. What other restraints do we need? However, we must submit ourselves to the three of these to see them accomplish their intended purpose.

CHAPTER 9

Soul vs. Spirit

Galatians 5:16-18: *Walk in the Spirit, and you shall not fulfill the lust of the flesh. 17 For the flesh lusts against the Spirit, and the Spirit against the flesh; and these are contrary to one another, so that you do not do the things that you wish.* NKJV

In these verses Paul points out that there is a struggle between the Spirit and the flesh, or the soul, of a believer. The illustration that comes to my mind is the old Disney cartoon with Pluto the dog.

On one shoulder is a little version of Pluto with a halo, angel wings, and wearing a white robe. On the other shoulder is a little version of Pluto with a pitchfork, horns, and a tail. Obviously, the one is encouraging him to do the right thing, while the other is prompting him to do evil. This is a good example of the struggle between the spirit and the flesh, which for the sake of this book is what I will regard to as the soul.

To understand what is being said we must first of all understand the makeup of man. Although the Lord our God is one, He exists in three distinct persons; Father, Son, and Holy Spirit. He is a trinity. Man has been created in His image; therefore, we are also a trinity, so to speak. We are made up of spirit, soul, and body. Our spirits are the non- physical part of our makeup that can connect or refuse to connect us with God. It is the very essence of our being. As already stated, we have all been born into this world with a spirit that is dead to the things of God because of the sin of Adam. When Jesus said we must be born again He was referring to our dead spirit.

Ephesians 2:4-5: *But because of his great love for us, God, who is rich in mercy, 5 made us alive with Christ even when we were dead in transgressions —*

The human spirit is the aspect of our being that has come alive at salvation; it has become one with the Spirit of God; it has been redeemed; it is holy and blameless and perfect in the sight of God. However, there is a problem with the soul. The soul (which is made up of our intellect, our emotions, and our free will) has not yet been redeemed, although at some point it will be. This is where the conflict comes in that Paul mentions in Gal 5. It wasn't till years after my conversion that I began to really understand what was happening with me.

I know there are many different interpretations regarding what Paul writes in Romans 7:15-25. Is this describing an unbeliever? Is this Paul's experience before he was saved? Is this Paul describing his life as a believer? Or is this describing the impossibility of a person living a godly life in one's own power whether saved or unsaved? For the sake of this discussion, I want us to consider this as Paul describing the ongoing conflict between the soul and the spirit that he mentions in Galatians 5.

Romans 7:15-20: *For what I am doing, I do not understand. For what I will to do, that I do not practice; but what I hate, that I do. 16 If, then, I do what I will not to do, I agree with the law that it is good. 17 But now, it is no longer I who do it, but sin that dwells in me. 18 For I know that in me (that is, in my flesh) nothing good dwells; for to will is present with me, but how to perform what is good I do not find. 19 For the good that I will to do, I do not do; but the evil I will not to do, that I practice. 20 Now if I do what I will not to do, it is no longer I who do it, but sin that dwells in me.* NKJV

Paul writes this epistle some twenty plus years after his conversion and admits that he has not reached perfection in his actions. He still sometimes does things he doesn't want to do and he doesn't always do the things he knows he should. I think if we would be honest, we would all have to admit to this same thing being true in our own lives. This is not describing someone who is in rebellion towards God. Paul says that he agrees that the law is good and in verse 22 he says, *For I delight in the law of God according to the inward man.* In his inner man, that is in his spirit Paul delighted in the law of God. He desired to do the right thing, but found himself sometimes not doing it. He goes on to say that he knows that nothing good dwells in his flesh (his soul). Thus, the conflict between soul and spirit. This was not a pleasant situation for Paul or for us.

Romans 7:24-25: *O wretched man that I am! Who will deliver me from this body of death? 25 I thank God — through Jesus Christ our Lord!* NKJV

The day is coming when we will see the consummation of our salvation; the redemption of the soul; no more wrong thoughts, no more stupid words, no more misguided emotions and also the receiving of our glorified bodies; no more aches and pains, no more sickness, no more death. Hallelujah! So, Paul points out here that he still does not always walk a blameless life, he still sometimes fails, he still sometimes sins. But he goes right from that into Romans 8:1: *Therefore, there is now no condemnation for those who are in Christ Jesus.*

In spite of our failures there is now no condemnation for those who are in Christ Jesus. Had I known this in the early days of my salvation there would have been a lot less anxiety.

CHAPTER 10

Obstacles to Grace

Colossians 1:6: *All over the world this gospel is bearing fruit and growing, just as it has been doing among you since the day you heard it and understood God's grace in all its truth.*

Paul commends these Colossian believers for their understanding of God's grace in all its truth. Unfortunately I have come to the conclusion that the majority of Christians do not have that same understanding today. Because of this many are living an inconsistent Christian life.

2 Corinthians 6:1: *As God's fellow workers we urge you not to receive God's grace in vain.*

First of all, we need to understand that Paul is writing this to the church, to believers, in fact he refers to them as God's fellow workers. Andrew Wommack states in his Bible Commentary that the word "vain" carries the idea of something that does not yield the desired outcome; something that is without effect or of no avail. (*Andrew Wommack Living Commentary*)

As I've considered this passage, I've concluded that there are several ways in which we can receive God's grace in vain. One way is in that we think it's not enough. Several years ago Barna Research Group did a survey among 6,242 believers or at least regular church attendees on whether there is additional works to be done in order to be saved apart from Christ's sacrifice on the cross; in the Assembly of God 22%, said there was need for more; Presbyterian 52%, Lutheran 54%, Roman Catholic 82%, Baptist 38% Methodist 59% Episcopalians 58%. When you average out these numbers it comes out to roughly 52%. So, then over half of believers or regular church attendees in America don't believe the sacrifice of Jesus is enough! So even amongst those who claim to believe there is the tendency to rely on one's own works and not really trust in God's provision. I believe we get a good illustration of this from ancient Israel. The prophet Isaiah warns the children of Israel that the Assyrians are about to come against them. But the Lord tells them not to try to make an alliance with Egypt but to simply trust Him.

Isaiah 30:1-2: *"Woe to the obstinate children," declares the Lord, "to those who carry out plans that are not mine, forming an alliance, but not by my Spirit, heaping sin upon sin; 2 who go down to Egypt without consulting me; who look for help to Pharaoh's protection, to Egypt's shade for refuge.*

Isaiah 30:15: *This is what the Sovereign Lord, the Holy One of Israel, says: "In repentance and rest is your salvation, in quietness and trust is your strength, but you would have none of it.*

Isaiah 28: 12-13: *He said, "This is the resting place, let the weary rest"; and, "This is the place of repose" — but they would not listen. 13 So then, the word of the Lord to them will become: Do and do, do and do, rule on rule, rule on rule; a little here, a little there — so that they will go and fall backward, be injured and snared and captured.*

Notice here that the result of them not listening to the Lord was that the word of the Lord became; Do and do, do and do, rule on rule, rule on rule. When there is no revelation of God's grace; when we don't trust in God's provision, then even the word of the Lord becomes rules and rules. God wanted His people to trust Him and not turn to man for help but they would not listen. The results of the Barna survey shows that same mindset is prevalent amongst many of God's people today. Although God has made provision for us to come to Him many within the Body of Christ still try to obtain acceptance through their own effort.

In Galatians 2:21 Paul says: *I do not set aside the grace of God, for if righteousness could be gained through the law, Christ died for nothing!"*

Contrary to popular belief; the greatest obstacle to God's grace is not sin, it is law, it is religion, it is actually in our trying to be good enough for God.

In his book entitled; There Were Two Trees in The Garden; Rick Joyner writes; *Satan is not threatened if we embrace the doctrines or the institution of Christianity; in fact, he may well encourage it. He knows that the good of the Tree of Knowledge is just as deadly as the evil and far more deceptive. Human goodness is an affront to the cross and is used as a compensation for it. It deludes us into thinking that if we do more "good" than evil, we will be acceptable to the Father, thereby placing us above the need for the sacrifice of His Son. Satan may well encourage us to embrace anything religious as long as we do not turn to the cross. (There Were Two Trees in the Garden; Rick Joyner)*

If we could gain acceptance with God through our works then Jesus died for nothing. God wants His people to rest in what He has already done. In Romans chapters nine, ten and eleven Paul draws a contrast between law and grace, works and faith and Jews and Gentiles.

Romans 9:30-32: *What then shall we say? That the Gentiles, who did not pursue righteousness, have obtained it, a righteousness that is by faith; 31 but Israel, who pursued a law of righteousness, has not attained it. 32 Why not? Because they pursued it not by faith but as if it were by works. They stumbled over the "stumbling stone."*

Romans 10:1-3: *Brothers, my heart's desire and prayer to God for the Israelites is that they may be saved. 2 For I can testify about them that they are zealous for God, but their zeal is not based on knowledge. 3 Since they did not know the righteousness that comes from God and sought to establish their own, they did not submit to God's righteousness.*

Romans 11:5-6: *So too, at the present time there is a remnant chosen by grace. 6 And if by grace, then it is no longer by works; if it were, grace would no longer be grace.*

Law or grace; you can't mix the 2 it's either 1 or the other. Receiving God's grace in vain not only leads to our trying to gain God's approval through our works and behavior, but it also keeps us from knowing our true standing before God. So what happens then is that we cannot enter into His rest.

Matthew 11:28-30: *"Come to Me, all you who are weary and heavy laden, and I will give you rest. 29 Take My yoke upon you and learn from Me, for I am gentle and humble in heart, and you will find rest for your souls. 30 For My yoke is easy and My burden is light."* NKJV

There is the story in Acts 3 where Peter and John heal a cripple at the temple gate called Beautiful. When the cripple saw Peter and John about to enter, he asked them for money. Then Peter said, "Silver or gold I do not have, but what I do have I give to you. In the name of Jesus Christ of Nazareth, walk." The point I want to make from this is that we can only give away what we have received. That same principle holds true as it relates to grace. If we have not received the revelation of grace, we are not able then to give it away. Unfortunately, the only thing that many unbelievers ever received from the church is judgment and condemnation. Years ago, several members of our church and I were involved in a motorcycle ministry. There is a large motorcycle rally held in our area every year called Thunder in the Valley. Tens of thousands of bikers show up from all over the East Coast. Once when we were there, we were right in midst of the festivities. There were dozens of vender booths and several hard rock bands playing. As we walked around, I began to hear someone shouting. As we got nearer to the sound, I saw a man standing up on a folding chair with a bullhorn screaming, "God hates you all, and you're all going to hell!" It wasn't exactly like the Day of Pentecost as there were not thousands being added to our numbers that day. I was surprised that none of those bikers went over and punched that guy in the mouth. In all honestly, I was tempted to go over and do a little laying on of hands. Yeah, I still struggle with the flesh by times.

One day as I was praying, I felt the Lord say to me, "You don't find grace anywhere in this world apart from Me." The message of grace is totally contrary to our way of thinking, because we live in a works based, performance based, behavior-based world. Not just as it relates to spiritual things but to life in general. Everywhere in life we are judged by some sort of standard. Remember there are no free lunches?

When we were in school, we were graded. Report card day usually wasn't a good day for me. I wasn't exactly an Einstein. I usually took the long way home from school on those days as I knew I would have to show my report card to my parents. Dad said, "What's with all the D's and F's?" I said that the school was now progressive and they were using a new marking system. The D's and F's meant doing fine. Yeah right!

In sports we're judged by how many points we can put on the board. That's why there is always a second and third string quarterback. They just don't live up to the standard of the starter. We're also often judged by the style of clothes we wear or even by the length of our hair. Several years ago, I was serving on a men's retreat weekend as a spiritual adviser. On Sunday afternoon at the close of the weekend a man who had attended came to me and asked me to forgive him. I had no clue as to what he meant. I said, "For what?" He said, "When they introduced you as a pastor on Thursday evening, I thought there's no way this long-haired freak can be a pastor; (remember I was a teenager in the sixties). He looks like the Tasmanian Devil. What a jerk! But then throughout the weekend I heard you share your testimony and listened to your teaching on God's grace and it changed how I saw you." Since that time, I have become close to this guy and have had the pleasure of seeing him grow in the Lord.

When I first came into the kingdom of God, I did not understand the magnitude of God's grace. I didn't understand that I was completely forgiven of my past and that there was now no condemnation for the sins of my present.

For several years I continued to struggle with the alcohol and drug thing. I would go for months without these vices and then run into an old crony and fall off the wagon. When I would fail I would literally weep thinking that God was angry at me. I would then actually start counting how many days it had been since I had failed. The longer period of time that went by determined how I felt about myself. In those times of failure, I would subconsciously go back to that painting of Jesus frowning down on me. At that point I thought, before I was saved, He hated me, now He's just thoroughly disgusted with me. At least I had moved up a rung or two on the acceptance ladder. Nothing could be further from the truth, but if you believe a lie, it becomes truth to you.

Joseph Prince often says that the way man looks at things is, "Do good get good, do bad get bad." Unfortunately, that is how we as believers often consider our relationship with God. If I'm doing good, God smiles on me and I have His favor but if I'm doing bad (sinning or failing) then He is not happy with me and in fact may be angry with me and send bad things into my life. It's like a spiritual daisy; He loves me, He loves me not, He loves me, He loves me not. Although this may be how we feel and think this is not what the Bible says.

Romans 4:7-8: *Blessed are they whose transgressions are forgiven, whose sins are covered. 8 blessed is the man whose sin the Lord will never count against him."*

Hebrews 8:8-11: *"The time is coming, declares the Lord, when I will make a new covenant with the house of Israel and with the house of Judah. 9 It will not be like the covenant I made with their forefathers when I took them by the hand to lead them out of Egypt, because they did not remain faithful to my covenant, and I turned away from them, declares the Lord. 10 This is the covenant I will make with the house of Israel after that time, declares the Lord. I will put my laws in their minds and write them on their hearts. I will be their God, and they will be my people. 12 For I will forgive their wickedness and will remember their sins no more."*

This new covenant does not just pertain to Israel as a nation but to all who would become the children of God.

John 1:11-12: *He came to that which was his own, but his own did not receive him. 12 Yet to all who received him, to those who believed in his name, he gave the right to become children of God—*

The word tells us that the Lord does not remember our sins and that He will never count them against us. This is because Jesus took our punishment, therefore there is now no punishment for us; He took the punishment we all deserve. If there is still punishment to be meted out to us, then what Jesus did didn't work. We have a hard time accepting this truth because it is so contrary to what we have been taught. But surely, His ways are not our ways. In the early days of my salvation, I did not understand this so when I would fail, I would beat myself up with guilt and condemnation. The problem was I didn't understand my position in Christ. I wasn't established in my righteousness.

CHAPTER 11

Our Identity

Romans 12:3: *For by the grace given me I say to every one of you: Do not think more highly of yourself than you ought. . .*

Here Paul warns us against pride. We're told in several places throughout the Bible that *"God opposes the proud but gives grace to the humble."* 1 Peter 5:5:

What I've come to realize over the years is that there is a flip side to thinking more highly of ourselves than we ought. That is thinking more lowly of ourselves than we ought. It is important that we be established in our identity. Something that came to me many years ago is the fact that Satan knows he cannot steal our salvation. So, what is the next best thing he can do? Render us useless for the kingdom of God. I believe one of the chief means of doing that is by getting us to doubt our identity in Christ. In the above verses we are warned against pride. I have seen very few believers rendered useless due to pride, but have seen numerous individuals who believed that God could never use them. The problem is that they believe a lie. They do not see themselves as God sees them. They live with a low self-worth being rendered useless in promoting the kingdom of God. In all honesty I struggled with this very issue myself for a number of years.

In Isaiah 54 there is a verse that I believe is often quoted out of context; verse 17 says: *No weapon formed against you shall prosper.* People use this verse to say that there is nothing negative that can come against them that can succeed. But if you back up a few verses you see the full context.

Isaiah 54:14-15: *In righteousness you shall be established; You shall be far from oppression, for you shall not fear; And from terror, for it shall not come near you. 15 Indeed they shall surely assemble, but not because of Me. Whoever assembles against you shall fall for your sake. NKJV*

Here God says there will be things that come against us, but it is not Him who is sending it. *Indeed, they shall surely assemble, but not because of Me.* He promises that He will not be the One who send attackers against His people. The word "established" used here means: to be certain, unchanging, firmly anchored, immovable, or enduring. In other words, "I shall not be moved!"

I want us to consider this passage as it relates to our identity. Being established in righteousness is understanding our position before

God; understanding how He sees us. It is having our foundation established. In relation to architecture, the foundation is the first step in building. It is imperative that the foundation be firmly established as the weight of the entire structure rests on it. Righteousness in the sight of God through Christ is the foundation of the Christian life; knowing who we are in Christ, knowing how God sees us. If we are established in righteousness, then; verse 17 tells us: *No weapon formed against you shall prosper, And every tongue which rises against you in judgment You shall condemn. This is the heritage of the servants of the Lord, And their righteousness is from Me," Says the Lord.* NKJV

I find it interesting that what rises against us in judgment is tongues. What has been said about us and to us throughout our lives and what do we even say about ourselves? I've come to the realization that these tongues that rise against us in judgment come from the world, our own flesh (our soul), and the devil. There is an old adage that says, "Sticks and stones may break my bones but words will never hurt me." That is a lie straight from the pit of hell. Not being a model student throughout grade school and high school I took quite a few beatings. I only remember a few. They never had any lasting effect on my life. However, some of the things that were spoken to me did have a lasting impression on me for many years.

It is not my intention to bash the Catholic Church; I am only sharing my own experience. When I was in fourth grade a nun told us that whatever part of our body that we sinned the most with would be the part that would burn the most in hell. "And, Kevin your tongue is going to burn." I was nine years old; this was a spiritual leader so I believed her. When I was in sixth grade, we went to Mass on a first Friday. The entire grade school went across the street to the church. Before Mass started another kid and I were talking and goofing around in our pew. A nun came up behind me, grabbed me by the hair, and almost lifted up me up out of the pew and shook me. She then just walked away. I sat there seething in a rage; she had just humiliated me in front of the entire school. At that moment I hated her with a passion. As I sat there, I looked up and there was Jesus frowning down on me. I thought, "Yeah, I know you hate me too."

For whatever reason I seemed to get into a lot of trouble when I was in the seventh grade. Once when the monsignor who was the principal of our school was scolding several of us, he said, "If you keep up this kind of behavior, I'm going to expel you." Another kid and I determined it would only be a matter of time before we got into trouble again so we decided we should just run away. As crazy as it may seem what led us to that decision was a story, we had seen on the Wonderful World of Disney which aired every Sunday night in those days. The story was of a little Mexican orphan boy who ran away from the orphanage he was in. With his little dog he crossed the Rio Grande and came into America. We figured if he could do it so could we. We decided we were going to go to New Mexico, so one snowy winter morning as soon as we got to school, we took off. We started to hitchhike, heading east. I guess we were going to New Mexico by way of New Jersey. We went about twenty miles until I decided this was stupid. It was cold and snowing, so I said, "I'm going back." He said, "I'm not." So, he was on one side of the road, hitchhiking east to New Mexico from Pennsylvania, and I was on the other side. Finally, a car stopped for me, I'll never forget it, it was a white 1958 Chevy Impala just like the one in American Graffiti. When my buddy saw a car stopped for me, he came over and jumped in with me. The guy took us the whole way back to school. As I started back to my classroom my dad who had been at the school office came around the corner and met me at the statue of Saint Michael. Bam! That was the only time in my life that my dad actually punched me. When we left school that morning the nun had immediately called our parents. My dad was working night shift in the steel mills so as soon as he got home my mom told him I had run away. So, he went out looking for me. It wasn't till years later that I understood why he was so mad. When I worked in the coalmine I told my four sons, "If you ever decide to run away don't do it when I'm working night shift." The rest of that school year was stressful; I was walking on egg shells afraid that I would screw up and get thrown out of school. I had no idea of what was to come.

As we began the eight-grade school year we got a new nun. This was her first and only year at the school. Rumor had it she was sent to a mental institution after that one year. On the very first day of school two other kids and I were talking before class. This nun went to the office and called our parents. ON THE FIRST DAY! In those days if the school called your parents, you were dead meat. That night my mom went off on me, screaming, "I wish you were never born!" I remember going out behind our house and sitting up on the grassy bank and crying. Now before you start to think that my mom was an ogre let me show you something the Lord pointed out to me years later. When we look at a person's behavior, when we see how a person acts, or how they talk do we ever consider why that person is the way that they are? Everybody has a story. Everyone is shaped in some way by the experiences of their past. My Mom was an angry person when I was young, and I didn't know why. But years later the Lord put it all together for me. In her youth my mom's dream was to become a school teacher. But when she was fourteen years old her mother died. There were fourteen children in her family, and my mom was in the middle. Her older siblings had married or at least had moved out. At that point my Granddad told her she had to quit school and take care of her younger brothers and sisters. She basically became the mother of seven children at the age of fourteen. She never went back to school, and her dream of being a school teacher died. I truly believe that situation had a major impact on her life. Her screaming at me that she wished I had never been born had an impact on my life for years. Even though I knew she didn't really mean it and it was just another one of her fits of anger, that thought seemed to lodge itself in my subconscious. It would be years before the Lord would set me free. From the very first day of school the eighth grade was a nightmare for me. I was so stressed out that my hair began to fall out. I ended up with a big bald patch on the left side of my head. My Mom took me to some kind of specialist. I don't know if he was a dermatologist, hairyologist or what, but I had to take these big horse pills (vitamins maybe?) and put some kind of lotion on the bald spot. Eventually my hair grew back. In fact, I think the reason I still have all my hair today was from all of that. A guy in our church told me one time, "You know when you're up there preaching, I can't help but think, man I wish I had a head of hair like that." Blessing in disguise.

Proverbs 18:21: *Death and life are in the power of the tongue,* NKJV

Eph 4:29: *Do not use harmful words, but only helpful words, the kind that build up and provide what is needed, so that what you say will do good to those who hear you.* GNT

Words have the power to build up or to tear down. A few years ago, my sister, Deborah, and I attended a Soul Care Conference. In one of the sessions, they were addressing family or generational issues. At one point, the speaker said, "Are there any particular sayings you often heard when you were growing up?" Deborah and I just looked at each other and laughed and said in unison, "What the hell's the matter with you?" We laugh at it now, but for many years I did think, "What the hell's the matter with me?" The point of all these examples is for us to consider how we see ourselves in light of our past experiences and what was said about us and to us. As we move on, we will see how the Lord sees us.

CHAPTER 12

Who Are You?

While man has the tendency to judge himself and others by behavior the Lord has a different standard.

Isaiah 55:8: *"For My thoughts are not your thoughts, neither are your ways My ways," declares the Lord.*

2 Corinthians 5:21: *God made Him who had no sin to be sin for us, so that in Him we might become the righteousness of God.*

Jesus was the sinless Son of God. He was not guilty of ever committing a single sin, yet He who had no sin became sin for us. This means that Jesus took on the sin of the entire human race.

Isaiah 53:5-6: *But He was pierced for our transgressions, He was bruised for our iniquities; the punishment that brought us peace was upon Him, and by His wounds we are healed. 6 We all, like sheep, have gone astray, each of us has turned to his own way; and the Lord has laid on Him the iniquity of us all.*

I personally believe that the Lord actually began to lay the iniquity of us all on Jesus in the garden of Gethsemane. That is why there was so much anguish. Can any of us imagine what that might have been like? Taking on the sin of the entire human race? The stress was so great that Jesus actually began to sweat drops of blood. This is actually a physical phenomenon known as hematidrosis.

God made Him who had no sin to be sin for us. When Jesus went to the cross, He carried the sin of mankind; that included yours and mine. So, when God the Father looked at Jesus on the cross, He saw our sin. But the rest of 2Corinthians 5:21 says; *so that in Him we might become the righteousness of God.*

So then, God the Father saw our sin on Jesus when He was in the garden of Gethsemane, when he was being scourged and when He was nailed and hung on the cross. But now as a believer when God the Father looks at us, He sees the righteousness of Jesus. It's like God says, "Let's make a deal! I'll take the punishment that you deserve for your sin and I will give you My righteousness." Jesus didn't have any sin of his own and we didn't have any righteousness of our own; He took our sin and covers us with His righteousness. How many of us then would be willing to say that we are holy and blameless and are as righteous as Jesus? 2Corinthians 5:21 says we have become the righteousness of God. We are covered by the righteousness of Jesus.

Why is it easier for us to believe that Jesus took our sin than it is to believe that we are seen as absolutely righteous in God's sight?

1 Corinthians 1:30-31: *It is because of him that you are in Christ Jesus, who has become for us wisdom from God — that is, our righteousness, holiness (sanctification) and redemption. 31 Therefore, as it is written: "Let him who boasts boast in the Lord."*

Isaiah 12:2: *The LORD, the LORD, is my strength and my song; He has become my salvation."*

Our salvation is not through religion, it is not by our good works, it is not by our behavior, it is not through doctrine or theology, or by going to church. I remember hearing the speaker at the revival in Brownsville Florida say, "You can go to hell in your choir robe with the waters of baptism dripping off your head holding your church membership certificate in your hand." Jesus has become for us our salvation, our righteousness, our wisdom, our sanctification, and our redemption. Our salvation is a person, it's Jesus. The way, the truth and the life. So, then what is our position with God? Who are we? What are we?

Ephesians 1:4: *For He chose us in Him before the creation of the world to be holy and blameless in His sight.*

We are holy and blameless in His sight because Jesus paid the penalty for our sin and covered us with His righteousness.

Colossians 1:21-22: *Once you were alienated from God and were enemies in your minds because of your evil behavior. 22 But now he has reconciled you by Christ's physical body through death to present you holy in his sight, without blemish and free from accusation—*

1 Peter 1:18-19: *For you know that it was not with perishable things such as silver or gold that you were redeemed from the empty way of life handed down to you from your forefathers, 19 but with the precious blood of Christ, a lamb without blemish or defect.*

Jesus was the perfect sacrificial lamb without blemish or defect.

Hebrews 10:14: *because by one sacrifice He has made perfect forever those who are being made holy.*

Several years ago, I was asked to speak at a men's conference. There were about one hundred and fifty guys there ranging from about sixteen to eighty years of age. I shared the Hebrews 10:14 verse and then asked for a show of hands to this question; Is there anyone here who is perfect? Only a few hands went up and that from a couple of guys who had heard me speak on this verse before. So, I read it again and asked the same question; again, almost no hands. So, then I said, okay, let's break this down. What is the one sacrifice that is being mentioned here?" Someone said, "The sacrifice that Jesus made." So, I said, "Is anyone here believing in that one sacrifice that Jesus made?" Almost everyone in the room put their hand up. I read the verse over again and asked, the same question "Is there anyone here who is perfect?" Once again almost no hands went up. It seems that we just can't bring ourselves to claim what God says about us. I think the problem is that we always look to behavior rather than to our position in Christ. We tend to look at what we do rather than on what Jesus has done. Through His sacrifice we as believers are without stain or wrinkle or any other blemish, but holy and blameless. This is how God sees us. Now the question might be asked, if we have already been made perfect through the sacrifice of Jesus how can we still be being made holy? We are perfect positionally before God, but we are being made holy or being sanctified according to some translations in our walk. None of us are living a perfect life

Romans 8:1: *Therefore, there is now no condemnation for those who are in Christ Jesus.*

There is now no condemnation; not when we die, not just in the future, but now! Unfortunately, very few believers walk in this truth. Instead, many live under condemnation, guilt and shame trying to perform in order to be pleasing to God. Regardless of what others may think about us or how we feel or think about ourselves, according to scripture this is who God says we are:

I am a son of God. (Galatians 3:26)
I am saved by grace. (Ephesians 2:8)
I am born of incorruptible seed. (1Peter 1:23)
I am redeemed by the blood of Jesus. (Ephesians 1:7)
I am forgiven of all my sins. (Ephesians 1:7)
I am a new creation in Christ. (2Corinthians 5:17)
I am redeemed from the curse of the law. (Galatians 3:13)
I am beloved of God. (Colossians 3:12)
I am an ambassador of Christ. (2Corinthians 5:20)
I am a citizen of the kingdom of heaven. (Philippians 3:20)
I am a joint heir with Jesus. (Romans 8:17)
I am accepted in the Beloved. (Romans 15:7)
I am free from condemnation. (Romans 8:1)
I am reconciled to God. (Romans 5:10)
I am justified by faith.(Romans 5:1)
I am qualified to share in Jesus' inheritance. (Colossians 1:12)
I am the temple of the Holy Spirit. (1Corinthians 6:19)
I am a saint. (Ephesians 1:18)
I am the elect of God. (1Peter 1:1)
I am established by grace. (Hebrews 13:9)
I am drawn near to God by the blood of Jesus. (Ephesians 2:13)
I am the righteousness of God. (2Corinthians 5:21)
I am a partaker of the divine nature. (2Peter 1:4)
I am delivered from the power of darkness. (Colossians 1:13)

I am forgiven of all my sin and redeemed through the
blood of Jesus. (Ephesians 1:7)
I am chosen of God, holy, and blameless in His
sight. (Ephesians 1:4)
I am perfect forever. (Hebrews 10:14)
I am as He is in this world. (1John 4:17)
I am complete in Christ. (Colossians 2:10)

There is no way in my natural thinking that I would have ever come to the conclusion that this is how God sees me. Truly, amazing grace!

Hebrews 11 is often referred to as the faith chapter. In that chapter there are eighteen individuals mentioned, these are put there as they are considered to be heroes or champions of the faith. But if you read the OT accounts of these individuals you see that out of the eighteen there are only four who lived what we might consider a godly life. The other fourteen were liars, murderers, deceivers, prostitutes, drunkards, scoffers and fornicators. Yet their past sins and failures are not mentioned here. They are all considered champions of the faith. Their acceptance by God was not based on their behavior or their goodness or their performance, but by their faith. This chapter is an illustration of God's grace. Grace is an attitude on God's part that proceeds entirely from within Himself, and that is conditioned in no way by anything in the objects of His favor.

CHAPTER 13

Knowin' Ain't Doin'

2 Corinthians 6:1: *As God's fellow workers we urge you not to receive God's grace in vain.*

As pointed out in the last chapter, the word "vain" carries the idea of something that does not yield the desired outcome; something that is without effect or of no avail. One way of receiving God's grace in vain is in believing that it is not enough as already discussed. Another way of receiving God's grace in vain is in believing that

71

as a believer it doesn't really matter what you do as you are already forgiven. The apostle Paul knowing human nature, knew that this would be the argument. In Romans 6 he addresses the issue.

Romans 6:1-2: *What shall we say, then? Shall we go on sinning so that grace may increase? 2 By no means! We died to sin; how can we live in it any longer?*

Romans 6:15: *What then? Shall we sin because we are not under law but under grace? By no means!*

Why would someone come to the conclusion that it is okay to continue in sin as a believer? Martyn Lloyd Jones once wrote this concerning grace; *There is no better test as to whether a man is really preaching the New Testament gospel of salvation than this, that some people might misunderstand it and misinterpret it to mean that it really amounts to this, that because you are saved by grace alone it does not matter at all what you do; you can go on sinning as much as you like because it will result all the more to the glory of grace. That is a very good test of gospel preaching. If my preaching and presentation of the gospel of salvation does not expose it to that misunderstanding, then it is not the gospel.*

I believe this misunderstanding comes from what Paul had already written in Romans chapter four.

Romans 4:4-8: *Now when a man works, his wages are not credited to him as a gift, but as an obligation. 5 However, to the man who does not work but trusts God who justifies the wicked, his faith is credited as righteousness. 6 David says the same thing when he speaks of the blessedness of the man to whom God credits righteousness apart from works: 7 "Blessed are they whose transgressions are forgiven, whose sins are covered. 8 Blessed is the man whose sin the Lord will never count against him."*

Since our relationship with God is not based on works but on faith then the assumption is that our works don't really matter. Furthermore, if we are forgiven and the Lord will never count our sin against us then what's the big deal? While we may be forgiven of our sin, we need to realize that there are consequences to our actions. Ephesians 4:27 says; *Do not give the devil a foothold.* In John 10:10 Jesus said, *the thief does not come except to steal, and to kill, and to destroy. I have come that they may have life, and that they may have it more abundantly.*

While the Lord may not hold our sins against us the enemy certainly does. His goal is to kill, steal and destroy. I have been involved in prison ministry for the past twenty years at a federal prison close to where I live. I once asked for a show of hands regarding the following question; How many of you were already a believer when you did whatever it was that got you put in here? About half of them raised their hand. Was going to prison God's punishment for their sin? No, prison was the consequence for their action. The enemy killing, stealing and destroying is prison, divorce, broken families, DUI's, depression, despair etc. all of these are the consequences of sin. These things are not the abundant life that Jesus wants for us. Satan wants to kill our joy, steal our freedom and destroy our families. These are actually self-inflicted wounds that come from bad decisions. I've come to the conclusion that prison is only one bad decision away. Since I have been ministering at the prison there have been state governors, mayors of large cities, pastors and counselors to the president confined there. While there is now no condemnation for those who are in Christ Jesus, how we as believers walk will have a definite effect on the quality of our lives. Even though we are not exempt from the troubles of this world we can certainly avoid some of them by how we live. My oldest son Nathan and I have had this conversation more than once. We've concluded that even if there was no after life, no punishment or reward, if this life was all there is, the quality of our lives has been so much better because of trying to live our lives according to the scriptures.

CHAPTER 14

The Administration of Grace

As we consider grace, we see that it is a multi-faceted jewel. There are many different aspects to the grace of God.

Ephesians 2:8 says that it is by grace that we are saved. Romans 3:24 says we have been justified freely by His grace. Titus 2:11:11-13 says that grace is the power of God in the believers' life to resist sin; *For the grace of God that brings salvation has appeared to all men. 12 It teaches us to say "No" to ungodliness and worldly passions, and to live self-controlled, upright and godly lives in this present age, 13 while we wait for the blessed hope — the glorious appearing of our great God and Savior, Jesus Christ.* And in 2 Corinthians 12:9 the apostle Paul says, *But He said to me, "My grace is sufficient for you, for my power is made perfect in weakness."*

Grace is the favor of God, but it is also the power of God. It is power over the effects of sin. Power for strength to overcome the obstacles in our lives, power to keep us from sinning and also the power to be His witnesses.

Ephesians 3:2-3: *Surely you have heard about the administration of God's grace that was given to me for you, 3 that is, the mystery made known to me by revelation,*

Ephesians 3:7-8: *I became a servant of this gospel by the gift of God's grace given me through the working of his power. 8 Although I am less than the least of all God's people, this grace was given me: to preach to the Gentiles the unsearchable riches of Christ,*

Galatians 1:15-17: *But when God, who set me apart from birth and called me by his grace, was pleased 16 to reveal his Son in me so that I might preach him among the Gentiles, I did not consult any man,*

Romans 12:6: *We have different gifts, according to the grace given us.*

1 Corinthian 3:10-12: *By the grace God has given me, I laid a foundation as an expert builder, and someone else is building on it. But each one should be careful how he builds. 11 For no one can lay any foundation other than the one already laid, which is Jesus Christ.*

1 Corintians 15:10-11: *But by the grace of God, I am what I am, and his grace to me was not without effect. No, I worked harder than all of them — yet not I, but the grace of God that was with me.*

So, Paul's testimony in a nut shell is that he was saved by grace, called by grace, given the revelation of grace, was gifted for the ministry of grace, and empowered by grace for the work of proclaiming the message of grace itself.

So, the Lord took an unlikely candidate (remember he hated Jesus and His people) and by grace raised him up to be one of the most influential individuals in the Christian faith. We see that principle throughout the entire Bible. God calls the reluctant and the unqualified to carry out His plans and purposes. Abraham was a liar; Moses stuttered, Gideon was a coward; Isaiah was a man of unclean lips; Jeremiah was too young; Samson was a womanizer, Rahab was a prostitute; Peter was a sinful man and Mary was a virgin; they were all unqualified! Then there was me. I was saved in 1979. From that point onward I thought I was pretty well set for life. By eighty-two I had four healthy sons. I had a wife that loved me. I had a good paying union job working in the coal mine; I had a mortgage, and a dog, I had the American dream. I figured this was what I would do for the rest of my life. God had other plans.

CHAPTER 15

Rev Kev

Having been raised Catholic and coming into the kingdom of God through the Charismatic movement in the Catholic Church I continued to attend the Catholic church for about three years. But one Sunday morning at Mass something happened. It was in the summer and it was very hot in the church. Then the priest said something that as a pastor I can't imagine ever saying; He said; "Look people I know it's hot in here; I know you don't want to be here; I don't want to be here either, so we're going to get this over as soon as possible. Mass was about twenty-five minutes long that day. I left there that day thinking there has to be something better than this.

From that point on we stopped going to church. But at that time on Sunday morning there were a number of television preachers that you could watch from six am to noon. This was on just regular network television; no cable, no satellite; just the big three. We watched Jimmy Swaggart, Rex Humbard, Charles Taylor, every week to name just a few. Then something happened that changed everything. We had a visit from some old friends Lenny and Elke that we hadn't seen for many years. Well, I fell off the wagon. Lenny and I started drinking about noon on Saturday and kept it up all day. By Saturday night we were pretty loaded. Sue was really mad at me and went to bed. Lenny passed out on the couch and Elke & I sat up talking. I was telling her about Jesus and how he changed our lives, Hiccup! Talk about God using the jawbone of an ass. (However, as a side note; two weeks later I got a call from Elke and she said, "Remember what you were telling me the other Saturday night about Jesus, well a lady at work was telling me the same thing and Lenny and I both got saved. That was the last of my drunken evangelistic crusade.) So, the next day they went home and I got the silent treatment from Sue all day. That Sunday night as I lay in bed I prayed; Lord send us to a church where we can learn and grow. The next day when I went to work a guy that I worked with every day and in fact a guy I had often went drinking and smoking weed with runs up to me and says; "Guess what happened to me? I got saved!" So throughout that day as we worked together, we talked about the Lord. At one point he said; "Where do you go to church?" I said I don't, so he said, "Why don't you come down to the church where I got saved?" I said what kind of church is it? He said, a Christian and Missionary Alliance Church. I said never heard of it; but it did hit me that I had just prayed the night before and here's this guy asking me to come to his church. He said I should come to the Wednesday night service and meet the pastor. This might sound stupid but I had no idea what a Protestant minister might look like. Maybe like Johnny Cash. I thought maybe he'd look like one of those preachers in the westerns I'd seen over the years. He'd be wearing a big black broad brimmed hat, a long tailed black coat and a string tie. Not quite. This guy comes in wearing a leather jacket, cowboy boots and carrying a motorcycle helmet. I had a motorcycle, and cowboy boots and was soon to get a leather jacket. I knew I had come to the right place. We ended up staying at that church for ten years. They weren't Charismatic or Pentecostal in any way but they were very Word oriented. I appreciated the years that we were there as we became grounded in the Word.

In nineteen eighty-five I attended a men's retreat weekend called Tres Dias. I know there is a lot of negative comments about it on the internet but if you've never attended a weekend don't judge it or criticize it. I have seen many people saved, revived, renewed and healed at these weekends over the past thirty-seven years as I have continued to serve. Tres Dias is a lay led ministry where ordinary believers from all walks of life and from all different denominations are given specific talks to present to a group of about forty men or women. There is a weekend for men and then the next weekend is for women. As I started giving these messages people began to ask me, "Did you ever consider being a preacher or a pastor?" Never! I had the American dream; I thought I was set for life. Through Tres Dias I began to get involved in prison ministry in one of the state prisons. Little did I know that this would go on for about thirty years. For several years as I got more involved people continued to press me about going into full time ministry. It was easy to blow off people but then the Lord got involved. I began to get this gnawing in my soul that I couldn't shake. But like all the champions of the faith in the Bible I had my excuse; (you know; I can't talk, I'm too young, I'm a man of unclean lips, go away Lord I'm a sinful man). Mine was, Lord I have no formal training, no education, I never went to Bible college or any college for that matter, I can't do this!

No exaggeration, the next time I flipped my Bible open it went directly to Acts 4:13: *When they saw the courage of Peter and John and realized that they were unschooled, ordinary men, they were astonished and they took note that these men had been with Jesus.* DANG! There went that excuse. Still, I resisted. Then one day I was talking to a guy in our church and I was telling him I couldn't just quit my job and go off to Bible school for several years, I had a wife and kids, a house and all that responsibility. To my surprise and chagrin, he told me, "You know the Alliance has a three-year Ministerial Study Program for guys like you who can't go to school full time." DANG! This program consisted of reading the required books, writing papers, meeting with an assigned mentor every month and getting more involved in the preaching, teaching ministry of the local church. At the completion of the course, I was then to enter into a two-year ordination program. I still struggled with this decision. One September night I was sitting out on my front porch wrestling with this whole thing. Suddenly SWOOSH a shooting star. Without even thinking I said, Lord if this ministry thing is what you want me to do I need to see another shooting star. SWOOSH, DANG! In one of the meetings with my mentor who was also my pastor at the time I told him of my concern for the future. If I have to go somewhere else to pastor a church, what am I going to do with my house; sell it, rent it? And what about my boys? Probably have to transfer to another school district; will it be in the middle of the school year; and what grades will they be in at that time? I'll never forget what the pastor said to me, "If this is what God has for you, He'll work out the details, I don't know how but He will work it all out somehow. You just have to trust Him."

So, in January of nineteen eighty-eight I began with the program. For the first two years I kind of kept up with the schedule but in nineteen ninety our pastor was out of the pulpit four out of six weeks with conferences and vacation. He asked me to fill the pulpit on those Sundays he was away. At that time, I was working six days a week in the mines. If I wasn't at work, I was at my desk preparing sermons. There was no time for family or anything else. I did it but decided this was too much, this wasn't for me, I decided to quit. I took all my books threw them in a box and put them in the closet. However, I never notified the district office that I quit. About three weeks later we went up to New York to visit Lenny and Elke. Sunday morning, we went to their church; the message was about Samson and how the glory of the Lord had left him without him realizing it. At the altar call the pastor said, "Maybe there's someone here today who is not doing what God has called you to do. I think almost everyone in the church went forward; including me. Okay Lord, I get it. I went home and did nothing. About a month later we went to Wisconsin to visit some friends we knew from when we lived in South Carolina. Sunday morning, we went to their church. The message that day was on the parable of the talents. What are you doing with what God gave you? I thought this guy must have been talking to that pastor in New York. So, I stayed in the program but I kind of dragged my feet. In nineteen ninety-one everything changed. I blew out three discs in my lower back at work and ended up on workers compensation for two years. When the doctor showed me the results from the MRI and indicated that I probably wouldn't be able to go back to work I was devastated. What am I going to do now? DUH! Because it was a work-related injury, I was referred to Occupational Vocational Rehabilitation. They were willing to pay for me to be retrained in another vocation. The guy interviewing me asked me what I wanted to do, I said I was already in a program to be a pastor. He just sat back in his chair and looked at me and said, "I've worked with hundreds of coalminers but I've never had one who wanted to be a pastor, but if that's what you want, I have thirteen million dollars I got to get rid of." I ended up enrolled in a two-year Pastoral Ministry course at the Reformed Presbyterian Theological Seminary in Pittsburgh. Not exactly a perfect match for someone who spoke in tongues. I would leave Monday night and come back home Friday afternoon. Meanwhile Sue was at home with five teenage boys, our four and one we had taken in. In addition to all of that she was going back to college to become a physical therapist assistant. It was a pretty crazy time. In July of ninety-three the pastor at Crossroads Alliance Church in my hometown of Ebensburg resigned and took a teaching position in Florida. Just as I began seminary in September I was contacted by the elders at Crossroads and asked if I would fill the pulpit on the Sundays that they weren't interviewing a perspective candidate. It ended up that I was preaching there almost every week. After about a month of this a friend of mine said to me, "Why don't you candidate there?" I said, I'm away all week at seminary, they don't want a pastor that's not around all week. He said, "All they could say is no." I just blew it off.

One Sunday around the middle of October as I was ready to leave the church one of the elders said to me, "Why don't you send your resume to the district?" I said what for? He said, "So that you can candidate here." I thought Humph, I would be nice to just stay right here in Ebensburg. But that's as far as it went. In all honesty I didn't pray about it or think about it much. At the beginning of November my friend asked me, "Are you still preaching there every week? Again, I said yes, he said, "Why don't you candidate there?" Again, I thought that would be good, and again I did nothing, no prayer, nothing. In the second week of November, I came home from seminary on Friday afternoon and Sue told me the district had called and that they were sending me a doctrinal questionnaire that needed to be filled out and sent back by the following Thursday. She asked them why, they said it was because they were tired of Crossroads calling them wanting me to candidate there. I filled it out and the following Thursday Sue and I drove to the district office and met with the Licensing and Ordination committee. As we drove along, I wasn't nervous at all as I thought to myself, I didn't do anything to make this happen. If this is God's plan then it's totally His plan because I haven't done a thing to make this happen. We were interviewed by eight pastors who had about one hundred and fifty years of ministry between them all. They put us out of the room for discussion and to vote on us. Shortly the chairman came out and said it was unanimous, he also said it was one of the best interviews he was ever in on. In early January I officially candidated and was voted in as pastor of Crossroads Alliance Church in my hometown of Ebensburg PA. Same house, same school district, same community. God had truly worked out the details just as my pastor had said years before. At the writing of this book, I have been pastoring at Crossroads Alliance Church for twenty-nine years.

Just as a side note. In His wisdom God knew He had to get me into the pastoral ministry without any effort on my part. Several times over the course of twenty-nine years there were times when I wanted to quit for whatever reason. Each time the Lord would say to me, "What did you do to get here?" Nothing, it was all You. He pointed out to me that if it had been by my effort, desire, choice or pursuit I could have used the excuse that I had made the wrong decision, "What was I thinking?" Throughout the whole course of my pastoral ministry God is the One who opened doors and sometimes closed them. It will be Him who closes the door for good.

Ephesians 3:7: *I became a servant of this gospel by the gift of God's grace given me through the working of his power.*

CHAPTER 16

Nothing but the Blood of Jesus

If you have read this far in this book hopefully you have a better understanding of the truth as it relates to your salvation. I have a note on my office door that says, "Assume Nothing, Communicate." So I'm not going to assume. I want to conclude with a few remarks about the Blood of Jesus.

Leviticus 17:11: *For the life of the flesh is in the blood, and I have given it to you upon the altar to make atonement for your souls; for it is the blood that makes atonement for the soul.'* New King James Version

Hebrews 9:22: *Without the shedding of blood there is no forgiveness.*

Amplified Version: *And without the shedding of blood there is neither release from sin and its guilt nor the remission of the due and merited punishment for sins.*

1 Peter 1:18-19: *For you know that it was not with perishable things such as silver or gold that you were redeemed from the empty way of life handed down to you from your forefathers, 19 but with the precious blood of Christ, a lamb without blemish or defect.*

Watchman Nee was a Chinese pastor who spent about twenty years in a communist prison. His comments on the Blood are some of the greatest ever written on this subject. In his book, The Normal Christian Life he writes;

The Blood is for atonement and has to do first with our standing before God. We need forgiveness for the sins we have committed, lest we come under judgment; and they are forgiven, not because God overlooks what we have done, but because He sees the Blood. If I want to understand the value of the Blood, I must accept God's valuation of it. It is God's holiness, God's righteousness, which demands that a sinless life should be given for man. There is life in the Blood, and that Blood has to be poured out for me, for my sins. God is the one who requires it to be so. God is the one who demands that the Blood be presented, in order to satisfy his own righteousness, and it is He who says; "When I see the Blood, I will pass over you."

If God can accept the Blood as a payment for our sins and as the price of our redemption, then we can rest assured that the debt has been paid. If

God is satisfied with the Blood, then the Blood must be acceptable. Let us remember that He is holy and He is righteous and that a holy and righteous God has the right to say that the Blood is acceptable in His eyes, and has fully satisfied Him. The Blood of Christ wholly satisfies God. (Watchman Nee; The Normal Christian Life)

What can wash away my sin? Nothing but the Blood of Jesus! If there is any doubt in your mind about where you stand with God and where you are going to spend eternity, I want you to carefully consider the following prayer. Before you pray it, though I want you to read through it slowly and truly comprehend what it is saying. Do you understand it? Do you believe it? And do you truly want this for yourself? If you do, then you need to pray it in faith out loud because in Romans 10:9-10 it says, *That if you confess with your mouth, "Jesus is Lord," and believe in your heart that God raised Him from the dead, you will be saved. 10 For it is with your heart that you believe and are justified, and it is with your mouth that you confess and are saved.*

A prayer of Salvation: Father God, I know that I have sinned and that I am in need of forgiveness. I believe that the sacrifice that Jesus made on the cross was done for me, personally. I believe that Jesus has paid the penalty for my sin. By faith I receive that forgiveness. Thank You Jesus for taking the punishment that I deserve. Fill me with Your Holy Spirit, lead me and use me for Your kingdom. In Jesus name.

If you prayed this prayer in faith from your heart you are now saved from the wrath of God. You are now indwelt with the Holy Spirit of God Himself. According to 2Corinthians 5:17 you are a new creature, the old has passed away, behold the new has come. Hallelujah!

BIBLIOGRAPHY

Chapter One: The Expositors Bible Commentary copyright 1986 by Zondervan Corp.

Chapter Four: Nelsons Bible Dictionary; Thomas Nelson Publishing Company.

Chapter Six: Vine's Expository Dictionary of Biblical Words, copyright 1985, Thomas Nelson Publishers.

Chapter Six: Aiden Wilson Tozer: The Knowledge of the Holy. Harper & Rowe Publishers copyright 1961.

Chapter Ten: Andrew Wommack Living Commentary 2008

Chapter Ten: Rick Joyner; There Were Two Trees in The Garden; Morning Star Publications 1992

Chapter Sixteen: Watchman Nee; The Normal Christian Life; Hendrickson Publishers Inc. copyright 1961

BIBLE REFERENCES

Unless otherwise indicated all scripture quotations are from the New International Version copyright 1973, 1978, 1984 by International Bible Society.

Scriptures marked NKJV are from the New King James Version copyright 1982; Thomas Nelson Publishers.

Scriptures marked NASU are from The New American Standard; The Lockman Foundation copyright 1977.

Scriptures marked AMP are from the Amplified Version; Zondervan Publishing House copyright 1965.

Scriptures marked GNT are from the Good News Translation; American Bible Society copyright 1976, 1992

Printed in the United States
by Baker & Taylor Publisher Services